"For every mom who feels spent, finished, bankrupt by bedtime. Eryn reminds us with humor, honesty, and relatable experience that what you spent in time, patience, energy, memories, and do-overs was worth every penny. Literally. The investment of a lifetime made by mothers everywhere. Every day. Often without even realizing it. Read on and take heart. Because every exhausted minute you've spent today was deposited in ways you may never have imagined."

—Lisa-Jo Baker, *Publishers Weekly* bestselling author
of *Never Unfriended* as well as *Surprised by Motherhood*
and *We Saved You a Seat*

"Every single month I find myself asking, 'Where did the time go?' And don't even get me started on holidays and milestones and new school years. It seems like no matter how hard I try to hold on to it, time slips through my fingers as my children grow up with increasing speed. If I let it, both accepting this reality or trying to change it can be overwhelming as a parent who desires to be intentional, to make a difference, to steward well the children God has given me. Thankfully, *936 Pennies* by Eryn Lynum is a resource any parent can use to replace confusion and chaos with purpose and value. If you are tired of looking back and wondering where the time has gone, this book will help you capture the moments God has given your family and make the most of your time together."

—Mary Carver, coauthor of *Choose Joy: Finding Hope
and Purpose When Life Hurts*

"Timeless, biblical truths combined with artfully crafted personal stories kept me engaged and desirous of learning more from this young mother, who is determined to use the time God gives her with her children wisely."

—Donna Keith, author of the children's book
I Love You All the Same

"What a beautiful and tangible reminder that each day with our children is a gift. It's very easy these days to squander our pennies. We're spending too much time texting, posting, and emailing, and so are our kids. *936 Pennies* will help you reclaim your days to invest in what really matters."

—Arlene Pellicane, speaker and author of *Calm, Cool, and Connected: 5 Digital Habits for a More Balanced Life* and coauthor of *Growing Up Social: Raising Relational Kids in a Screen-Driven World*

"As a mother of two adult daughters, I thought to myself while reading *936 Pennies*, *Where was this book while I was raising my girls?* I love the heart of Eryn as she took the charge from her pastor to intentionally build into her children's lives. And now, as the reader, you will reap the rewards of her obedience to savor the moments we are given, with practical tips and honest struggles."

—Jessie Seneca, speaker and author of *Raising Girls Diaper to Diamond*

"*936 Pennies* reminds us time is a priceless but not limitless gift. Eryn Lynum invites the reader to join her quest to be intentional in the way time is spent while raising children. Her words are tender and her message is compelling. This book is a parenting treasure."

—Lori Wildenberg, licensed parent and family educator, speaker, author of four parenting books including *Messy Journey: How Grace and Truth Offer the Prodigal a Way Home*

936 Pennies

Discovering the *Joy* of Intentional Parenting

Eryn Lynum

BETHANYHOUSE
a division of Baker Publishing Group
Minneapolis, Minnesota

Published by Bethany House Publishers
11400 Hampshire Avenue South
Bloomington, Minnesota 55438
www.bethanyhouse.com

Bethany House Publishers is a division of
Baker Publishing Group, Grand Rapids, Michigan

Printed in the United States of America

Library of Congress Cataloging-in-Publication Data
Names: Lynum, Eryn, author.
Title: 936 pennies : discovering the joy of intentional parenting / Eryn Lynum.
Other titles: Nine hundred thirty six pennies
Description: Bloomington, Minnesota : Bethany House Publishers, [2018] | Includes
  bibliographical references.
Identifiers: LCCN 2017037306 | ISBN 9780764219788 (trade paper : alk. paper)
Subjects: LCSH: Parenting—Religious aspects—Christianity. | Parenthood.
Classification: LCC BV4529 .L96 2018 | DDC 248.8/45—dc23
LC record available at https://lccn.loc.gov/2017037306

Cover design by Kathleen Lynch/Black Kat Design

Author is represented by Leslie H. Stobbe

19 20 21 22 23 24 25   8 7 6 5 4 3 2

To our Savior, Jesus.
Author of time and giver of hope.

To Grayson.
Your belief in me has taught me to soar.

And to our children.
You show us every day
how to best spend our 936 pennies.
You amaze me.

Contents

1. Counting Time

The Jar 15

First Pennies 19

Uprooted and Overhauled 24

2. Amplifying Time

Insatiable Cravings 31

Nature's Classroom 36

Strawberry Juice 41

Amongst the Waiting 47

Laugh Lines 52

3. Slowing Time

We'll Trade Our Whole Life Away . . . 61

Boredom Blocks 66

Derailed 71

A Hot Cup of Resentment 75

The Plan That Changed Everything . 79

Chamomile Tea 84

Tire Swings 89

4. Speaking of Time

Callous Words 97

This Is Who You Are 103

"We've Got This" 109

5. Standing the Test of Time

Depleted 115

"How Did We Do It?" 119

Chisel 124

6. A Perspective on Time

Out of Control 131

The Shattered Jar 138

Their Stories Matter 142

Resting Secure 147

Unwavering Faithfulness 152

7. Navigating Time

Desperate for Answers 159

"Was This the Right Move?" 165

Not-So-Expert Advice 171

Promised Land 178

8. Preserving Time

Stones and Gems 187

Chapters 190

From Humdrum to Holy 193

Cemeteries and Stream Beds 197

The Gift of Their Own Stories 201

Handing Over a Legacy 206

9. **Buying Back Time**

    Reclaiming 205 Pennies 213

    What's in Your Child's Hands? 219

    Resetting Our Default 223

10. **Timeless**

    "Be Brave, Little One" 231

    Supermoons and Small Love 236

    The Full Jar 240

    Acknowledgments 245

    Notes 247

-one-

Counting Time

The Jar

My teeth were clenched as I balanced our frantic toddler on my hip, discreetly stuffing animal crackers into his mouth. It was a desperate attempt to keep him focused and quiet, and it was failing. We had missed his nap-time window, and it was backfiring big-time. Our three-year-old stood next to my husband. He stared out into the crowd, tightly clutching his daddy's hand. The sight of him caught me off guard, exceptionally handsome in his light blue button-up shirt and dark denim jeans. He looked much older than his three years. It was a rare occasion when our family looked so put together, but it was all about to unravel at the whim of our one-year-old, Ellison. He thrashed about in my arms, struggling to break free from my grasp. I repositioned him on my hip so that his kicks would be directed away from my midsection. Our third son was nestled deep within my abdomen—a secret shared between my husband and me.

We stood on a stage with a handful of other families from our church. It was Child Dedication Sunday, and we were there to vow, in front of our church family and God, to raise this unruly boy on my hip to know and love the Lord. It was an important day for us. "Down! Down! Down!" Ellison yelled at the top of his little lungs as he pushed my hand away. *Five more minutes. We only need to keep it together for five more minutes,* I silently prayed.

Our pastor introduced each family. He then turned to the parents onstage and reminded us all of the great responsibility we have to raise these children into godly men and women. He reassured us of the support we would have in our church family. The congregation then bowed in prayer for the children and for the mission before us to show them who Jesus is. The bowing of heads seemed to be the clincher for my son's waning patience. Any last scrap of civility he had was now gone. He wailed through the entire prayer. With our pastor's "amen" came a few snickers from the crowd. The laughter was good-natured; our church family understands the wildly unpredictable temperament of toddlers. But my face was still flush with embarrassment as we found our way offstage, my flailing toddler in one arm and a small gift in the other.

Gifts are often given at these child dedication services. At our former church, where I worked as the assistant to a children's pastor and was responsible for putting together these gifts, we gave away children's worship CDs and kids' Bibles. But nothing would prepare me for the gift I was given on this day, at our own son's dedication.

As our pastor spoke to us on the stage that morning, he had given each family a glass jar full of pennies. My hands dropped a bit as I took in the full weight of the jar; it was heavy with the weight of exactly 936 shiny copper pennies. "In these jars is a penny for every week you will raise this child," our pastor explained. And with his words, the jar felt exponentially more heavy in my grasp. "Every week, when you get home from church, remove one penny from the jar. It will be a reminder of the time you have left to raise your child before he or she goes out on their own." I stared at the pennies, all shiny and glinting inside of the glass jar. They looked like so many . . . yet so very few.

Our pastor instructed us that upon bringing our jars home, we should begin by removing a penny for each week old our child was. Ellis was one and a half. He was the oldest child being dedicated that Sunday morning, and I had a lot of pennies to remove. So many, in fact, that weeks later I had not removed a single one of them. Maybe it was because I hadn't carved out a spare moment to sit and count them out. . . . But I suspect it was because my heart was afraid to feel the weight of seventy-six pennies being emptied from that jar, never to return. Perhaps I was afraid to begin removing pennies because I knew that with each penny I removed, that little glass jar would only grow heavier, more imminent, and more immediate. It wasn't only Ellison's jar that was weighing heavy on my heart. When I looked at our firstborn, now three years old, my soul felt the weight of 172 pennies gone. I had to ask the inevitable question: How had we spent them?

In Ephesians 5:16, God's Word tells us to make the best use of the time, because the days are evil. "Teach us to number our days," Moses prays in Psalm 90:12, "that we may gain a heart of wisdom." Removing pennies from a jar is exactly this: time counting. It is us numbering our days, that we may gain a heart of wisdom. Is that not what every one of us parents yearns for along this journey: a heart of wisdom in how to spend this time?

Countless things have changed in the arena of motherhood since the very first birth story, when Eve welcomed baby Cain into the world. But two things have not changed. One is the reality of the limited time we as parents have with our children before they enter into adulthood. The other is the responsibility we have as parents to use that time well, to nurture and shape and guide our children into an abundant life. Nine hundred and thirty-six weeks is what we are given, and sometimes not even that many. Too many parents know the unspeakable grief of having those weeks cut short. We are never guaranteed the time we have with our kids. In light of that, our responsibility grows all the more imminent to spend that time fully. Our new jar of pennies was a stark reminder of this.

For weeks that jar sat on the floor in the backseat of our car. I could hear it *clink-clinking* as it rolled back and forth between tiny race cars and sippy cups when I would accelerate from or pause at a stop sign. I avoided it, along with the weighty task it challenged me to. I avoided it until one day I could avoid it no longer. Leaving the jar untouched would not make time stand still. I reached underneath the driver's seat and brought the jar inside. I set it on my desk and stared at it for a few minutes before walking to the kitchen in search of another. Rummaging through my canning equipment, I found a glass mason jar, this one empty, yet full of potential. I set it next to the jar of pennies. This new jar represented the investment of a lifetime—truly, the investment of an eternity. Every morsel of the time that we have with our children we are called to grab hold of and use it for showing our children exactly who Jesus is. This is when I began to count.

I counted out seventy-eight pennies. They represented the weeks we had spent with Ellison since first bringing him home from the maternity ward. As I counted them out, I placed them into the new jar, and this is when it hit me—*we had not lost those weeks*. We had used them. We were using them for the creation of something beautiful. These pennies, and the weeks they represent, were not being cast to the wind. They were being invested. And we wanted to invest them wisely.

First Pennies

Parenthood is full of waiting. We wait for the plastic test stick to reveal a positive sign, or perhaps the referral letter from the agency an ocean away. We wait for the first kicks within our abdomen, or the doctor to speak "boy" or "girl." We wait for the home visits and paperwork and court date. Some of us, caught entirely surprised by that positive sign, wait and hope for the shock to give way to excitement. Some of us wait for the ultrasound and that tiny heartbeat to release us from our deepest fears. Some of us wait for years.

And yet nothing can prepare us for that day when we take our first step over the threshold into parenthood. No matter how many birthing classes we attended or parenting books we pored over in recent days, despite the heaps of advice we've been showered with, when that child is first placed into our arms, we find ourselves very ill-equipped. And there we are, tasked with figuring it out as we go, moment by moment, day by day, week by week, some of us wondering if we'll ever truly *figure it out*.

We may think that the countdown ends when the umbilical is cut or the adoption papers are finalized, but that is exactly when a new clock begins to tick away at time. We stare down at our new child, hoped for and prayed for and altogether perfect in our eyes. And this is when we fall under the full weight of our new responsibility. Wrapped up in this child is so much potential, and it is in that moment that we begin to understand just how much of our child's future and well-being rests in our hands. Staring at a newborn baby, eighteen years feel so big. Staring at a jar of 936 pennies, the same amount of time holds a deep sense of urgency.

However we enter into parenthood—whether completely expected or utterly surprised, with a perfectly orchestrated birth plan, an emergency C-section, or a labor of paperwork to bring a child home from across an ocean or across the state—here is this child and here are we, together: a new and beautiful unity. Nine-hundred and thirty-six weeks, if that, stretches out before us. And the question must be asked: How will we spend them? Will we choose to feel the weight of time passing, and if we do, how will that change today and tomorrow?

This is the challenge of counting time. We must choose it. We must choose the feelings, challenge, urgency, and mission—and it hurts. Moving that penny every week is a heavy task. But we choose this work of counting time because it asks us the difficult questions that ultimately guide us into a fuller life for us and our children. Every week as we move a penny to our "invested" jar, it leads me to ask myself questions like these:

- How did I invest this week in a manner that will impact my child's future?
- What did we do this week that invited laughter into our home?
- How did we invest time in our child's creative spirit this week?
- How did we intentionally slow down this week?
- How did I show my child Jesus this week?
- What priorities and values did I model to my child this week?
- What do I need to ask my child's forgiveness for?

Penny counting begs that these questions be asked. The weight that we feel each week as we unscrew that metal cap and move a penny from one jar to the next—we cannot do this without feeling. We cannot do it without consideration. We cannot do it without asking the questions that really matter, the ones that will shape our child's life, as well as ours. And as we count, as we ask, as we answer, we discover the beauty in these days. We learn to pick them apart, dissect them, behold them, and be grateful for each and every one of them and the lessons they hold within. We discover that there is room and grace for our mistakes. Moving these pennies has taught me that God's grace is so much larger than all of my tongue slips and raised-voice regrets.

> We choose this work of counting time because it asks us the difficult questions that ultimately guide us into a fuller life for us and our children.

Perhaps that is the greatest lesson that counting these pennies teaches us: Jesus is enough when we are not.

Right before Moses died, he gave these words to Joshua, next in command, and they are true for us today: "The Lord is the one who goes ahead of you; He will be with you. He will not fail you or forsake you. Do not fear or be dismayed" (Deuteronomy 31:8 NASB). Every week, no matter how demanding and exhausting, God has promised you His presence, and that is everything you will need for walking this road of parenthood. No matter your situation, He knows it, and He is waiting to meet you right where you are. He goes before us, and He already knows what lies ahead. He knows the way. That is the beauty of these penny jars—they reveal to us just how much we need Jesus for this journey.

The truth is, when I stare at that jar of pennies, it is not only a poignant reminder of time's limit. It is also a reminder of my own limits. Some days I feel I am squandering our time together. With one slip of the tongue, one impatient reaction, or one missed opportunity to speak truth, I wonder if any of this is doing any good. A penny can be invested; it has the potential of growing in value. It also has the potential of getting lost in a couch cushion. The time we have with our children holds the same potential. Each moment is an opportunity to teach and to be taught—to love, to nurture, and to shape our children. Within these moments is when we show these little ones who Jesus is and what the value is of following Him. And I have discovered in my own motherhood that this is only possible when I myself am resting at the feet of Jesus and living in light of the promises in His Word. We discover freedom and hope in parenthood when we choose to see ourselves as Jesus sees us—forgiven, free, and righteous.

He calls us righteous, yet we feel anything but that. Parenthood acts as a mirror—and one of the most unforgiving kind—that reveals every little blemish and imperfection that we might have never noticed before. Where in the midst of our everyday challenges as parents can righteousness find a place? It is in our second penny jar that I see this question begging to be asked. This is the jar where we keep the pennies that have already been invested, the ones we have already spent. They speak of time and choices. They look tarnished; blemished by human touch and marred by my own faults. The ones in that first jar—still waiting to be invested—look shiny and new. And I wonder if there is any way to transfer them from one jar to the next without smudging them by my shortcomings. It's easy to feel wholly unworthy of investing these pennies.

Where is righteousness in all of this mess? It is in Christ alone.

"God made him who had no sin to be sin for us, so that in him we might become the righteousness of God," says 2 Corinthians 5:21. And in 1 Peter 3:18, "For Christ also suffered once for sins, the righteous for the unrighteous, to bring you to God."

But there is one caveat. We find it in the 2 Corinthians passage: "That in Him *we might* become the righteousness of God." God's grace leaves little room for conditions, but here we see it—that little word that we get caught up on: *might*. There is a possibility of leaving all of the promises—our hope for abundant life and intentional parenthood—sitting on the table to collect dust. For days. For months. For years. For decades. For a lifetime. For your child's lifetime. For generations. Far too many legacies are made up of dust.

This one condition—the one thing holding us back from the life we so desperately desire for ourselves and our children? The condition itself is adorned in grace. "For I am not ashamed of the gospel, for it is the power of God for salvation to everyone who believes. . . . *For in it the righteousness of God is revealed from faith to faith*, as it is written, 'But the righteous shall live by faith'" (Romans 1:16–17 NASB, emphasis added). Here it is, a promise wrapped up in ribbons of grace, accepted through the practice of faith—the act of believing. All that is required of us is the acceptance of the gift and promises laying before us; a receiving of this free gift through faith.

That gift of promises sits waiting on the table with your name scrawled across the gift tag. You glance down, the package glimmering in the light. Promises of abundant life for you and your family. There are traces of blood on that gift—the holy blood of Christ shed for us on the cross. This gift was bought with a price, and now it is given away without one, *"to everyone who believes."* When we accept this gift, Christ's blood spreads over us to make us completely clean before His eyes. Not just for heaven, but for now. He sees us clean *now*. Forgiven of our harsh words yesterday, our impatient reactions today, and our slip-ups tomorrow. He looks down upon us and sees only the blood—only Christ's righteousness on our behalf.

This is where we see it—what we dared not imagine before—that we can be righteous. *Right now.* Christ himself is our righteousness. Only when we realize this—His perfect and complete provision on our behalf—can we begin to grasp the promises that He gives us in His Word. And those promises, made fully available to us right in the mess and chaos of everyday parenting, provide everything that we need to invest our pennies well.

Uprooted and Overhauled

If it is possible to break a bone with a sippy cup, then my son had just accomplished this feat. Out of the corner of my eye I saw it coming. However, flying sippy cups are a pretty common occurrence in a house with young kids such as ours, so this instance caused me no alarm. He raised the plastic ammunition high above his head and readied it for the launch. I subconsciously braced my ears for the sound of plastic hitting the hardwood floor, but I kept on with the conversation I was having with my husband. We were used to talking above the clatter by now. That's when shock hit. I stopped speaking midsentence as pain reverberated from the second toe on my left foot all the way up to my hip. I yelled—loudly. And then I yelled again; both times in pain. My mind did a quick analysis of the situation to see if it warranted my next action. It did not, but I went ahead anyway, driven by the pain and anger. I yelled a very choice four-letter word. Yes, right there in front of my three-year-old and one-year-old. Now a whole different kind of shock reverberated through me.

Immediately I felt tears welling up in my eyes, but not from the surprising pain caused by the sippy cup. No, these were the tears of shame, the kind not unfamiliar to parenthood. Because parenting can often be wracked by moments of failure, ugly reactions, bitter words, and regret. Parents are made up of the same fallible nature of all human beings, and raising children can bring out the ugliest parts of us.

Before we ever enter the realm of parenthood, people tell us how hard it will be. They'll tell of sleepless nights and toddler tantrums, of teething and fevers, of bullies on playgrounds and difficult friends, of teenage rebellion and first dates. But the knowledge that not many of us walk into parenthood equipped with is just how much raising children will strip us of ourselves. We come into this job wholly unaware of how deep our anger can burrow, how loud our voice can raise, and how short our patience can run. And when those dark parts of us make themselves known in the quickest of moments, we reel back, feeling completely exposed for who we never knew we were.

It has been in these darkest moments, when anger evolves from a simmer to a boil, that I realize just how needy I am in this journey.

Have you come to a point where you feel as though you have run completely out of patience? Are you out of energy and out of kind words? Maybe you question whether you're cut out for the work of raising your children. This can be a very lonely place, leaving you uncertain of where to turn, and wondering if anyone notices just how desperate you feel.

> Have you come to a point where you feel as though you have run completely out of patience? Are you out of energy and out of kind words?

It was in the midst of this discouragement that I came face to face with the complete overhauling of my motherhood. It was not at all where I expected to encounter the uprooting of my foundation. However, tucked into the book of Proverbs, I discovered everything I hadn't known I was searching for, and it was the hope I was fiercely longing for.

It is hardly a passage that parenting magazines or sermons visit often. In fact, it makes little to no reference of raising children. Yet strung throughout three short chapters in Proverbs, my heart found room to breathe under the weight of my discouragement. The power of these verses is found not in prescriptive advice in how to raise our kids, but in the address they make to our own hearts. Before we can ever expect to find freedom in our call and rise above the guilt of our shortcomings, we must first take account of our heart's state.

Nestled into chapters ten through twelve of Proverbs, the author, Solomon, paints a contrast between a righteous and an unrighteous person. As he does so, he strings together a list of promises for the righteous person. He writes of blessings on the head of the righteous and calls the mouth of the righteous a fountain of life. He speaks of legacy, naming the memory of the righteous as a blessing to others. In Proverbs 10:16 we read that the work of the righteous leads to life. And I find in these words that one of my deepest prayers as a parent has been answered: *Lord, all of this work, all of this toil and heartache and early mornings and late nights, let it lead to life.*

In verse 24 we read that the desires of the righteous will be granted. Their hope brings forth joy, and they speak what is acceptable—no four-letter words on the account of a perilously tossed sippy cup, I'm sure. It was as I read this passage through the lens of my own motherhood that I began seeing these promises as more than lofty ideals, but rather as the truths in which Jesus wants us to find freedom. It is why He came, after all, to save us and become our righteousness, and to make these promises available to us.

● ○ ● ○

As a parent, the desires for my family and our future run deeper than the baby sleeping through the night or straight A's on a report card. I want my family to have an everlasting foundation. I want my children to remain unshaken when they walk through hard seasons of life. I want them to reap from their life what is beautiful and worthy of their time, because they sowed what is good with the moments they've been given. I want them to desire what is pure and full of peace. I want them to have confidence that their desires will be granted, because what their heart longs for has aligned with what God's heart wants for them. I want my children to "flourish like a green leaf" (Proverbs 11:28 ESV), to think upon that which is just and to bear fruit that will bring life to others. As we read through the promises of the righteous person in Proverbs, I don't see a list of unattainable character traits. I see the plea of a mother or father writing out any and every desire of their heart for their parenthood, children, family, and legacy. I see a declaration of how every parent wants to see their time spent during these 936 weeks—on that which is worthwhile and everlasting.

These are the promises we long to be true of us and our families. And no matter how stuck or hopeless we feel in our current reality, God's Word tells us these promises are for us. They are His gift, the equipping and enabling of us as fallible humans to take on this high calling of raising the children He has given us. These are the promises that, once we let go and fully embrace, will uproot and overhaul our doubts and discouragement. They stand in the way of any notion that we can do this on our own. Instead, they offer a new foundation for us to stand upon and a new roadmap for us to navigate the days we have been given to raise our sons and daughters. But first we have to step off the platform that was home to our self-sufficiency that never was quite enough. We have to take the first step and free-fall straight into the safety net of these promises, trusting them to catch us.

In this list of promises I catch a glimpse of the most gracious and stunning parenthood I could ever dream of. *In these verses we find the heartbeat of time, and how it was meant to be invested.*

Wherever you stand (or lay collapsed in exhaustion) in your parenthood journey, take heart. As we read in Proverbs 12:7, we *can* see our house stand; and in 10:25, our family firmly established upon an unshakable foundation. These three little chapters overflow with the promises that we long for as parents. We *can* walk securely. We *can* be a fountain of life for our children. We *can* see our deepest desires granted for our family. We *can* be a witness of hope, bringing joy to our children. We *can* be delivered from the trouble around us. We *can* speak what is good and acceptable. We *can* be guided by integrity.

Whether you are nuzzling the soft newborn hair of your first child, or you are sorting through college applications with your high-schooler, now is the time to ask yourself this all-important question: What would change in yourself and your family if you were to claim these promises as your own? Now let this truth sink in deep; let it take root and begin to flourish and birth hope. Let it steep within your soul and simmer in your heart. These promises can be yours.

Yes, there will be days when we lose sight of them. As distractions and discouragement battle for our attention, we will forget to claim these promises as our own. It is not an overnight transformation, but rather a lifelong journey to discovering what it means to live with our identity rooted in Christ. But we must always return to this truth: These promises are for us and for our children. And they hold the power to completely uproot and overhaul the course of our lives and redirect our 936 pennies in a magnificent manner.

Questions to Reflect On

- How might your view of time shift if you saw it not as something being lost, but rather as something being invested? Regardless of time already spent, how would this change your heart and actions moving forward?

- Are you viewing your parenthood through the lens of mistakes and regrets, or through the lens of Christ's love and grace? What promises from His Word could transform you as a parent?

- In your mind, what specifically does it look like for your child to "flourish like a green leaf"?

-two-
Amplifying
Time

Insatiable Cravings

I couldn't believe he asked it. This was the same question he had been asking for weeks. Before, it was cute. Now it only made me angry. We had delivered on our promise, yet he was asking for more. Perhaps you, like I, have wondered when your child will ever learn to be content and to stop asking for more. Or maybe you've asked yourself if you went wrong somewhere; if your child has not learned how to be grateful for what they have. Little did I know that, in this case, my son had a lot to teach *me* about being thankful.

My head was foggy, the bright sun a harsh reminder of my coffee deficit. If we did not find a coffee shop soon . . . well, let's just say that things were going downhill quickly. My husband, Grayson, and I had woken fatigued and cranky from our road trip the day before. We had spent ten hours in the car with our three young boys, stopping every couple of hours so that I could nurse the baby. Now, rubbing groggy eyes and packing snacks into our bag, we drove up into the breathtaking mountain town of Estes Park, Colorado. Our boys were all but bouncing in their car seats with anticipation as we made our way through the canyon framed by jagged, steep rock faces, and ascended up into the Rocky Mountains.

Grayson and I settled into wooden Adirondack chairs next to a duck pond at the local coffee shop. Grayson bounced our four-month-old on his knee as we relaxed with our coffee. Our two older boys busied themselves with tossing corn kernels to eager ducks. That is when Zeke came to me with his question. "Mama, can we go to the mountains now?" I stared at him for a moment. Then I glanced from his yearning eyes to the mountain peaks towering up to the clouds all around us. Luminous green pine trees and aspens just beginning to transform into golden hues stood tall on the mountains surrounding us.

"Zeke . . . we *are* in the mountains," I told him.

"But, I want to go to those mountains!" He pointed high up into the pine forests and jagged rock faces at elevations I was certain one would require climbing gear to reach, not to mention a level of courage I lacked.

"But, buddy," I scoured my brain for an explanation that might satisfy his young and longing heart. "We are *in* the mountains. Do you remember that we had to drive way up here, and we kept going higher and higher? Well, now we are in the mountains!" He hardly looked satisfied with my answer.

His question would be a constant tension in my neck throughout our entire vacation. As we drove mountain passes up into the Horsetooth Reservoir, and up further still into the great elevations of Breckenridge, Colorado, he would ask each time, "Mama, when can we go to the mountains?" Again and again he would point higher up to intimidating summits eclipsing the clouds above. No matter what altitude we took him to, he wanted to go higher still. He wanted more. We were doing it right, or so I thought, to bring them here to this beautiful place. After all, taking a vacation with three little kids is hardly restful and hardly affordable. My husband and I had made the small sacrifices in order to invest our time with our kids well. Why was our son so ungrateful? Why did he always want more?

The psalmist describes it as a "wanton craving" (Psalm 106:14). God had masterfully delivered His people from the hand of the Egyptians. He had provided absolutely everything that they needed. He had performed miracles right before their eyes. And yet they had this insatiable craving for more. The Psalmist points out, "Our fathers, when they were in Egypt, did not consider your wondrous works; they did not remember . . . your steadfast love" (Psalm 106:7 ESV).

Those first few days in the mountains, I heard my son's insistent requests for more, and all I saw was a bad attitude. I boiled it down to a relentless discontent and a lack of appreciation for the beauty surrounding him.

It wasn't until halfway through the week, on a desolate desert path, that I finally began to understand my son's discontent as more than a wanton craving. My husband had pointed out the trail a few days earlier, and today he had encouraged me to go and explore it by myself. I strapped on my running pack, tied on my shoes, and took off down the path. My Midwestern lungs were unacquainted with the thin air of Colorado, and I figured that I would turn back at the first loop of the path. The trail wound along a harsh red rock wall that towered high with ragged edges pointed at the sky. It was a type of natural barbed-wire fence, a barrier between the city and the foothills of the Rocky Mountains. I arrived at what the map called the Keyhole. It was a natural window in this rocky fence; a frame around a breathtaking view of the great Rocky Mountains. This was the turnaround point, and yet the trail was beckoning me to continue. There I stood, with the path to the right leading back to the parking lot, and the path to the left winding down into a valley, then up into a steep ascent on the other side. My skin was hot and turning red under the sun's rays, and my lungs were struggling against the altitude. But I could not stop. I turned left and began running down into the valley. As I rounded every corner, I found myself taken aback with complete wonder and awe.

> This is when I finally got it. I understood my son's relentless desire for more. His longing was far greater than the type of wanton craving of the Israelites. It was a holy kind of discontent.

"Wow." I whispered it through exhausted breaths as more mountain peaks made themselves visible with my climb.

I wanted more.

This is when I finally got it. I understood my son's relentless desire for more. His longing was far greater than the type of wanton craving of the Israelites. It was a holy kind of discontent. I had so much to learn from him. It was not that he wasn't impressed with the mountains that week, it was that he *was* impressed—and he wanted more.

Zeke had seen it with his own eyes, just what that the psalmist penned in Psalm 111:2: "Great are the works of the Lord; they are studied by all who delight in them" (NASB). He was delighting in the works of the Lord, and his young heart was yearning for more of this majesty, for more of this beauty. The Hebrew roots of the word *studied* in this verse paint a picture of *pursuit*. It means to seek out with a sense of urgency or demand. That is exactly what my son was doing. He was in pursuit. He had glimpsed God's masterful creation, and it had left him with a holy discontent, an insatiable longing for more of his Creator. He wanted to spend more time in more of God's creation. This is exactly how children study the works of the Lord: they play among His creation. Children seem to have an innate understanding of how God created us to spend our time in worthwhile ways. We have a lesson or two to learn from them in this area.

Scripture says that exposure to God's creation leaves us with no excuse in coming to know Him as God. "For since the creation of the world God's invisible qualities—his eternal power and divine nature—have been clearly seen, being understood from what has been made, so that people are without excuse" (Romans 1:20). This is why I pray that my children will always have an unyielding longing to experience more of God's creation, because it leads them right into the arms of their masterful Creator. And, just as the psalmist penned in Psalm 95, I understand that amidst God's magnificent creation is where my children will be ushered into a life of praise and worship.

In his hand are the depths of the earth;
  and the mountain peaks belong to him.
The sea is his, for he made it,
  and his hands formed the dry land.
Come, let us bow down in worship,
  let us kneel before the Lord our Maker!

Psalm 95:4–6

Nature's Classroom

When we expose our children to God's creation, we plant within them a holy discontent and a desire to experience more and more of their masterful Maker. I have come to realize that if we are going to spend our 936 pennies well, then we must spend a good portion of them outside, where our children will glimpse the splendor of God's creativity. A mountain trail, an aspen grove, or the sea-salt wind of the ocean may be all it takes to sow within our children an abiding longing to discover the One who holds the depths of the earth in His hands.

Maybe it is difficult for you to join your children playing outside because there is so much to be done inside. The dishes won't wash themselves, after all. Maybe you are simply not the outdoorsy type, preferring an afternoon curled up inside with a good book. Believe me, I understand. That sounds heavenly to me, too. Yet it is not enough for me to send my children outside to play when they grow a little too loud for the house. Investing my time with my kids outside requires something more—it requires my presence. The outdoors provides one of the richest classrooms I have for teaching my child about who God is. Early Christian author Tertullian said it: "Nature is schoolmistress, the soul the pupil; and whatever one has taught or the other has learned has come from God—the Teacher of the teacher."

Moses, when imparting God's commandments to the Israelites, said this:

Hear, O Israel: The Lord our God, the Lord is one. You shall love the Lord your God with all your heart and with all your soul and with all your might. And these words that I command you today shall be on your heart. You shall teach them diligently to your children, and shall talk of them when you sit in your house, and when you walk by the way, and when you lie down, and when you rise. You shall bind them as a sign on your hand, and they shall be as frontlets between your eyes. You shall write them on the doorposts of your house and on your gates.

Deuteronomy 6:4–9 ESV

As parents, we are given the task of telling our children about Jesus. We have the great privilege of explaining to them just how wonderful God is, and all that He has done for them. We are called to do this not only during bedtime prayers. We need to weave words of grace and biblical truths throughout the fabric of our days, and what better opportunity to teach our kids about their Creator than by walking side-by-side with Him in the beauty of His creation?

Nature provides us the perfect classroom for teaching our children about God's provision, protection, and how He makes all things new. After all, Jesus used sparrows to show us that God will give to us all that we need. He used sand and stars and strands of hair to show how deeply and fully He knows us and cares for us. He used grass and flowers to show us how fleeting time is, and that our lives are but a breath of air. He used a mustard seed to teach how great the kingdom of God is. He used soil and wheat and sheep and a fig tree. And He has given us all of these teaching resources at our fingertips, if we'll only take a walk outside with our child.

The truth is, I have struggled with this. I did not always appreciate spending time outside. In fact, my attitude toward the outdoors caused some consternation between my husband and me early on. You see, our relationship began on a lie.

My husband is the outdoorsy type. I fell head over heels in love with Mr. Rugged and Adventurous. He had been a mountain climbing guide in Colorado and grew up more or less as a child in the woods while his parents worked at camps. Grayson loved everything water, everything climbing, everything fast, and everything risky. He never grew out of that, a fact for which I am very grateful today. Early on when we began dating, he explained to me his annual tradition of going tent camping on the coldest night of the year. We were in Wisconsin. Believe me, the coldest night of the year is *cold*. It's the type of cold you can't shake from your bones even hours after returning home. It's the type of cold I would rather believe not exist as I remain inside, cozied up next to the fireplace. He loves this cold. I most certainly did not. But sometimes in the bliss of a new relationship, we believe that we can re-create ourselves a little bit. Back when Grayson and I were still wooing one another toward the altar, I let him believe a lie. In my defense, I had conned myself into believing it first. I decided that it might not hurt to portray myself to him as the woman I thought I could be. After all, I was smitten. And so when he asked, I told him, "Yes, of course I'll go camping with you and your friends come the coldest night of the year!"

As the temperatures began to drop, I sensed that the day was at hand. His anticipation grew, and the glimmer in my eyes quickly faded to fear—and to second thoughts. When the day finally arrived and he announced that we were headed out to the woods with a tent that evening, I spoke a resounding "No." This would go down in our relationship history book as "The Argument." This is also when I am sure he began to sense a sort of lie, that perhaps I wasn't so in love with the outdoors as I had made it seem. That maybe the glint in my eyes when he spoke of adventure and roughing it was a bit of a facade. Perhaps if he had stared a bit deeper into those eyes, he would have sensed some deceit. It was not that I didn't like the outdoors. It's just that I *really* liked being warm on a cold night. And a comfortable sofa. Fortunately, my bad attitude did not wear on my husband. His appreciation for nature would engrain itself within me. And then when we became parents, I would find myself with every reason in the world to be outside.

It all took place a few years into our marriage when our first son was learning to stand and walk. The first time Zeke stood up, we were at a friend's farm picking beans straight from their vine. I looked over to see my son gingerly raising his tiny body into a stand. His plump little hands slowly pulled away from the ground, and his unpracticed legs shook a bit as he straightened out his back. My hands ceased from their rhythmic motion of picking beans, and I stared at him. His sun hat was strapped under his chin, and one leg of his plaid overall shorts was hiked up to reveal his chubby thigh. He looked at me to make sure I was watching. *Yes, my boy, I'm seeing this!* A few months later I would observe him as his soft little feet navigated through green grass for the first time. His eyes grew wide, fully expressing the surprising sensation of the blades slipping between his toes. That is when I fell in love with being outside. Every new discovery, adventure, and accomplishment among green grass, pine trees, and beach sand was a grand experience to him, and to me.

Our boy was captivated with creation, and I was captivated by his wonder at it all. As we welcomed our second and eventually third son into our family, I no longer fought spending the bulk of our days outside. At first I tolerated it. But very quickly the allure of God's creation wound its way around the deepest parts of me. As I witnessed within my children a great appreciation for and fascination with nature, I had to ask what I was seeing. I soon learned: I was seeing worship.

> Going outside was becoming an act of worship for our family.

Childlike faith often looks like our sons and daughters simply enjoying who God is and what He has made. And going outside was becoming an act of worship for our family.

Whether you consider yourself a person who enjoys the outdoors or not, we owe it to our children to give them the opportunities to come to know their Creator through what He has made. It need not be a large ordeal, maybe a trek through mountain trails or a weekend camping in the backcountry. I've seen it happen on the most unassuming of walks along a dirt path. Or under the syca-more trees next to a favorite playground. Or within a few minutes standing outside under a starlit sky. The smallest sips of creation have a way of impressing profound memories into our children's hearts. And you never know—among these small exposures to the wonder of all that God has made, you might just find yourself falling in love.

Strawberry Juice

There is a plot of land, just shy of an acre in size, sitting on the outskirts of Kansas City, Missouri. It was not much to speak of, but that little spot was home for two years. We had rented up until that point in our marriage, and this was our first time owning a home. I fell in love with it for the yard. When our Realtor took us to see the house, I walked the fence line, leaves crunching beneath my shoes, then whispered to my husband, "This is it. I want this one."

It was a magical patch of land, a bit of a surprise to find in the middle of town. The yard was canopied by large, mature sycamore trees. They would sway back and forth over my boys as they played, their leaves bright green in the summer, golden yellow in the fall. There was a small patch of dirt in the center of our yard, and the boys claimed it as their play place. Every day that little mound of dirt would transform into a construction area. As the sun would make its leisurely voyage across the clear blue sky, nonchalantly signaling the passing of hours, the boys busied themselves with projects made of mud and rocks. Trucks, trains, and cars carried loads of mud on rainy days, or loads of dusty dirt on dry days, filling, loading, dumping, then repeating for hours. There is something therapeutic about running your hands through earth. This is one thing my sons taught me as they would coax me to come sit in the dirt next to them.

On one particular afternoon, with the boys fully entranced in their latest construction project, I busied myself in the garden. I was lacing bean vines through their climbing fence, encouraging them on their ascent toward the sun. I looked up to discover the boys' construction site abandoned. I turned toward the garden gate that they were heading to. Our youngest had just turned one, and he was crawling after his big brother. I knew what they were after. I joined them at the strawberry patch and ran my hands through leaves in search of bright red berries, ready to satisfy my boys' excited taste buds. I pointed one out to our oldest, Zeke, and showed him where to place his feet between the strawberry plants. He bent down and carefully positioned his fingers around the plump red berry. He plucked it from the stem and handed it to me. "Clean, Mama?" I removed its green top, wiped it of dirt, and handed it back to him. He popped the juicy morsel into his mouth and immediately began scanning the patch for another. As I helped him locate another ripe strawberry, I heard the *pop* of a berry being pulled from its stem. I turned around to find Ellison admiring his newly picked berry. He had successfully found a ripe strawberry, delicately removed it from its stem, and popped the entire treat into his mouth. He, too, turned back to the patch in pursuit of another. As berries still warm from the sun filled their mouths, joy filled my heart.

That evening before bed I did as I have done every night since I became a mother. I knelt at my son's bedside and, as he took deep breaths, sound asleep and unaware of my presence, I prayed over him and kissed his soft forehead. As I rose to leave his bedside, he grabbed my hand tight to pull me back. I could tell he was still mostly asleep. His eyes remained clasped shut as he mumbled something in his sleepy state. I couldn't decipher his words and softly began to pull my hand away. He grasped it tighter as he repeated his sleepy words, but this time I could make them out. His words stopped me in my tracks. "Pray strawberries, garden?" his sleepy voice asked. I lowered my forehead to touch his and grasped his hand tightly in my own. "Thank you, Jesus, for the strawberries in the garden." How is it that the prayers of a child have such a way of reminding us of what is truly important in life?

I squeezed his hand once more before turning toward the door, and as I did, I whispered my own prayers of thanks. I thought back on the day marked by dirt under my fingernails and not a whole lot crossed off the to-do list. I thought about mud trailing along the bathroom floor, and shoes scattered by the back door. And then I thought about strawberry juice slowly slipping down boys' chins—and I gave thanks.

That is exactly what spending our days outside does—it evokes gratitude and appreciation. It teaches us just how beautiful life is when we take time to notice the details and live in awe of God's creativity. Our children have a unique, innocent way of bringing us straight back into that classroom of discovery, if only we'll follow them into their outdoor adventures. When we surrender our own agendas, stop faking interest, and instead enter ourselves fully into our child's delight with outdoor play and discovery, we rediscover a childlike faith. A faith that says, *Yes, this is enough. This flower, that sparrow singing in the tree, that reflection of the mountains in the lake—yes, God is real.* In this way, we move from showing our child who God is, to our child reminding us of His grandeur and majesty. When parenthood brings with it questions and hurts that cause us to doubt our very faith, our child points to the sunset horizon or the full moon casting its glow on the backyard, and we remember, *Yes, God is big. God is good. God is loving.*

● ● ● ●

A lot has changed in our world over the past few generations. Spending our days outside has become an anomaly. What was once normal and even expected behavior has now become strange. Screen time, constant activity, and plain old busyness have squeezed outside time from our agendas. It is our job as parents to place nature back in its rightful place, so that our children learn that time spent outdoors is an integral part of living an abundant life. It is our job to protect and nurture their innate craving for outdoor play and wonder, lest they ever lose sight of that allure and stop chasing after their Creator amongst His creation.

It all begins with us as models. It takes us digging, climbing, running, jumping, and exploring, so that our children will know that although the times have changed, and although it might seem strange to some, spending our days outside is an act of worship to the God who created us for enjoying His masterpiece. Our children meet God in a whole new way when they meet Him outside. They learn to praise God in tune with all of creation.

> Let the heavens rejoice, let the earth be glad;
> let the sea resound, and all that is in it.
> Let the fields be jubilant, and everything in them;
> let all the trees of the forest sing for joy.
> Let all creation rejoice before the Lord.
> Psalm 96:11–13

We have lived in places where nature was plentiful and easy to find. We have also lived in areas where it was more difficult to come by. Whether you live nestled within mountains, among farmlands and fields, or in the middle of a city, God's wonder is begging to be explored. It can be an afternoon drive to a nearby park, an impromptu trip out of the city to glimpse the stars shining against the night sky, or a stroll along the river. That is the thing about God's creation. Even amidst the developing world, His creation stands out, if we'll only set our mind, eyes, and hearts to finding it.

Blue skies and cotton-ball clouds have become an irresistible invitation for me to play outdoors. They beckon, and there is little that can hold me back from basking in their God-given glory. It's on one of these days, when cloud shadows dance across green grass and the sun is kissing the sycamore trees just right, that we decide to stop for a picnic lunch on the way home from church. We unload the boys at one of our favorite playgrounds. As quickly as we can unclip their seat belts they are off and running to conquer new heights on the playset. My husband positions a picnic table under the shade of a large oak tree. I nestle our newborn son under his nursing cloth. The boys return from their play every few minutes to munch on cheese and grapes. When the baby finishes his own lunch, I lay the nursing cover across the picnic table and gently lower him onto his back. He gazes with eyes wide open up into the trees, watching bright green leaves sway and dance with the wind.

My husband clears the table and heads off to play with the boys. I gaze down at my boy. At two months old, everything is still brand-new to him. And he is still brand-new to me. I watch him, taking him in as he takes in the world around him. This is the world that I want him to know. A world of clay dirt ground and white-bark trees. A world of adventure and discovery and worship. A beautiful world. The wind picks up, a perfect breeze complementing the heat of the sun. As it blows across his tiny body, he writhes with excitement. His long, thin limbs wave back and forth, and his little eyes open and close rapidly at the whims of the wind. The wind is a new sensation on his delicate skin, and his whole body expresses the wonder of it all. I caress the soft skin of his tiny calf muscle, moving down to massage his bare toes. He continues to dance in the breeze.

I'm finding more and more that this is how we take in the wonder of creation—through children. Whether it's through the prayers of my eldest from the strawberry patch, or the dance of my newborn taking in the sensation of the wind, they teach me what it is to stand in awe of God's artistry. No longer can I let it go unnoticed, because they force me to stop and take it in. No longer can I say no to that blue sky and its marshmallow clouds. I must heed their call and dance in their glory, offering back praise to the One who crafted them, and also crafted my family and me for the enjoyment of them.

> When we spend our days doing exactly what God crafted us to do—living in enjoyment of Him—time is amplified.

We only have so much time. Those penny jars sitting on our shelf serve as a constant reminder of this. And yet, it appears that we can manipulate time. Or rather, that when we spend our days doing exactly what God crafted us to do—living in enjoyment of Him—time is amplified.

As we invite our children to walk down a mountain path, stand before the ocean, or count the stars, we invite them to know their Creator in an intimate way. And when those children are grown up, the pursuits that they choose to chase after will be hugely impacted by how many of those pennies we spend amongst the evergreens and sunflowers. Let's give our child every opportunity to taste and see that the Lord is good, and to know the One who created every beautiful thing outdoors and called it good, and then created them and called them *very* good.

Amongst the Waiting

Twenty-two months of my life were spent with my husband and our firstborn son. We had those ninety-five weeks to pour into our oldest boy before we would bring a brand-new swaddle of life home. My husband worked as a roofer during that time, often leaving before the sun came up and returning home long after it had set below the horizon, working tirelessly to provide for this little family we had made. I could not have known it then, but that time was a rare and priceless opportunity to pour into my firstborn. Never again would I have so much time to invest individually into one of my children.

When our second boy came along, we had to get a little bit more creative in finding time to spend one-on-one with each of our boys. But we still made it happen. When the boys didn't synchronize their nap times, I would find an hour here or there to spend on the floor playing with just one of them while the other slept. On occasion, my husband would take one boy out on a Saturday morning and I would keep the other home with me. But then our third son arrived, and we found ourselves outnumbered. I had heard more than a couple of times that going from one child to two was very difficult, but that going from two to three was a breeze. However, we found this to be altogether untrue. Between changing diapers for three children, nap times that never took place at the same time, and sleepless nights, I was hard-pressed to find a moment to myself or for just my husband and me, let alone time to spend one-on-one with each child.

This is why, when I found myself alone with our youngest son at 11,000 feet sitting on the edge of a crystal clear mountain lake, my first instinct was to freeze that moment in time. At fifteen months old, Weyland had hardly mastered walking, yet here he was maneuvering his tiny sandaled feet across the pebble-bottomed stream bed. My husband sat on the opposite side of the lake, perched halfway up a mountain ridge. Our two older boys, five and three at the time, busied themselves running between us on the dirt path that wound around the lake. After not spotting them for a few minutes, I yelled over to my husband. "Grayson!" His name echoed across the lake, nothing else to be heard except the soft trickle of water in the stream next to us and Weyland's playful giggles. My husband stood and pointed, and I followed his finger and caught a glimpse of our boys' heads popping up over a hill. They were holding hands and heading back toward Daddy.

I turned back to our youngest and watched him bend over and splash his little hands in the water, squealing with delight as he looked back at me, making sure I was watching. I was. And I soaked in every bit of him, from his sandy ankles to the water droplets dancing on top of his eyelashes. It was the first day of our family vacation. We had left our house a few hours before and still had several hours before we could check into our cabin. And that is what found us sitting beside this lake nestled between towering mountain peaks. I locked eyes on my boy, whose eyes were locked on a chipmunk watching us from across the stream. That's when it hit me again: we weren't killing time, we were stretching it.

We parents feel it so harsh and relentless—the passing of time; this force of such great strength that we feel we cannot control. We want to hold it, savor it, capture it, cherish it. And yet it slips through our fingertips, as if sand in an hourglass. We will that sand to stay at the top. *Please just wait, let me hold you, child, in this moment, just a little while longer.* But then we glance back at photos from last year's vacation, or we watch a video from the first weeks home from the delivery room or the orphanage—we compare those pudgy faces and little voices to current time—and it strikes us just how much time has passed. It won't slow down, and its speed can be terrifying.

Three months after that afternoon at the mountain lake, where I watched our youngest splash in the stream at 11,000 feet, we would return to that same place. We would glimpse that lake, now ice covered, and this time with my parents, brother and sister, and niece and nephew in tow. We would all stand together, shivering and all smiles, at the sign marking 11,990 feet. Snow-capped mountain peaks towered behind us. We'd snap a photo of all of us together, and I would stare at that photo and see it—generations of memories. I would picture my boys, years from now, all of our pennies spent, remembering that moment with all of our family—all of us present, fully there with one another. And in that moment, we cheated time. We stopped it. We stretched it out and filled it full with all of the love and togetherness that it could hold. Time held no power over us because we were holding it right in our hands—telling that morsel of time in our history exactly what it was meant for.

Perhaps one of the greatest angsts in our hearts as parents is the knowledge of how short our time is. When I speak to other parents about the message behind those penny jars, I see a visible response. Removing pennies hurts, and it is supposed to. A constant reminder of the shortness of time is meant to stir up a response within us. As the psalmist penned it, "Teach us how short our lives really are so that we may be wise" (Psalm 90:12 icb).

Teach us how short our lives really are. This is what time counting is all about; this is the message held in those penny jars. The realization of how limited our time truly is—the knowledge is heavy. It's something we don't like to think about. But we do. And we talk about it every time someone tells us, "Enjoy it, the time goes quickly!" *Oh, we know.* I am sure I will know it more fully when all of our pennies are spent. But even now, with partly spent jars, I know it well. And this knowledge, although heavy on my heart, is a gift. *Teach us how short our lives really are so that we may be wise.* Out there sitting next to a mountain stream, watching our boys run and laugh and enjoy the fresh air breathed out by the One who spoke them into existence—that is wise spending, because after our pennies are all spent up, those times when we chose to freeze time by spending it outside—those are the pennies that I will remember.

When outside, children lose all sense of time. There is no schedule or agenda. There are only sticks, rocks, flowers, mystery, and discovery. And out here, as we watch our little ones lose themselves in wonder, we also are free to lose all sense of time. Or rather, perhaps we will become keenly aware of it, fully cognizant of its power and just how rich it can be; we can discover its fullest potential. In the rush and bustle of daily life, time becomes small, lost among the chores, routines, habits, and agendas; out here, time becomes big. It expands. It must, for it has so much more wonder and awe to hold. Out here, we see time as it was meant to be, fully appreciated for the gifts it brings us, if we'll only afford it our full attention. If we'll only stop to admire the honeybees gathering pollen from wildflowers and the water droplets dancing atop a toddler's eyelashes.

● ○ ● ○

It does not only happen on the mountaintop. Stretching moments into memories can take place every day, wherever we find ourselves. At the kitchen sink kneading dough next to little hands eager to help. On our morning commute to drop the kids off, as we talk of life and dreams and ambitions. On an impromptu trip to the ice-cream shop after dinner. Each penny holds so many moments, and so much opportunity to cement those moments into a childhood full of meaningful connection. Every day is an invitation to attune our hearts to a slower pace of life and to lose our sense of time.

Many times, these opportunities are found amongst the waiting of life. So much of life is spent waiting. It is how we see the waiting that matters. It is how we choose to use the waiting, how we find beauty in the waiting, and how we create beauty in the waiting. And whether we'll arrive at the end to look back, only to realize that throughout the waiting, we did a whole lot of living. It is within those pockets of waiting scattered across our days that we can amplify time, stretching it out and filling it with memories that our children will carry with them into adulthood.

I write these words from a bed-and-breakfast nestled on the shore of the Puget Sound. Friends of ours run this quaint little blue-and-white house, welcoming in strangers, homing and feeding them, then bidding them farewell as friends. But on our visit, our friends are not here. They are across the Puget on the mainland, waiting. They wait in a hospital room to welcome their brand-new baby boy.

Meanwhile, their young son and his grandma hold things down at the bed-and-breakfast, and I sense their waiting. I can feel it in the air, hovering over me, melding with the aroma of warm blueberry muffins and tea. Grandma talks about the new baby brother. Big brother asks questions. They wait. We all wait. And as we do, I think back to those times in my own life. Three times have we waited in those hospital rooms, eager and anticipating. I can recall the vivid details of those times

Stretching moments into memories can take place every day, wherever we find ourselves.

waiting; within them, moments found room to flex and stretch and become more than they appeared. Time itself stretched. Not only because I was so eager to hold our boys, but because I was fully aware of the awe in those moments. I knew their magnitude. The waiting was beautiful, and memories nested within that will last me my entire life. Today they wait on a baby. I wait on words to come. Yesterday we waited for the ferry to bring us to this island. The fishermen down on the water wait for bites. Life is threaded together by these snippets of time spent waiting. And although the waiting often tempts us to ask time to speed up, it is actually our invitation to slow time down—to lose sense of its passing, and weigh it down with our presence.

Laugh Lines

The ceremony was over. All of the guests had moved into the auditorium—the one I coached kindergarten girls' basketball in, the one I set up tables for youth events in, the one I ran with toddlers on Sunday mornings in, the one with those terribly bright lights that we spoke of in staff meetings and how they skyrocketed the church's electricity bills—and now the one that held my wedding cake. The guests sat around tables adorned in black and deep teal, with a live fish nervously dancing in a small bowl at the center of each table. The nerves surrounding the ceremony had passed, but I was still a little apprehensive about the toasts. What would my father say to this man who had just taken full responsibility for his youngest daughter? I knew he would be kind, but my father is a little bit . . . unpredictable, at times.

(Two years later he would stand up again to give away his oldest daughter—my sister. He would turn to the guests and explain that he had been given the responsibility of presenting the father's toast. He would then proceed to pull from his suit jacket pocket a piece of bread—crispy-edged white bread that he had scorched with a blow torch just before the ceremony. My father's "toast." It epitomized his sense of humor.)

Understandably, I was a little suspicious about what he would say at my wedding, what words of wisdom he would have for the man who would now take care of me. He began by looking at my mother. He pointed out her laugh lines, those thin lines that run so elegantly from the outside corner of each of her eyes and inch gracefully toward her hair. He took full responsibility for them. "They are from years of laughter," he explained. Her face grew flush as every eye at the reception turned to her. I loved how my father honored her. My heart smiled; I could picture so many of those moments that inscribed those laugh lines onto her face—I had been present for many of them. My mother's laughter, the sound of it imprinted deep within my soul through its ever-present residence in our home and in my heart. He made her laugh—every single day. And my life was richer because of it. My dad turned back to my new husband and gave him this charge: "Make her laugh every day. Be the one to create those laugh lines around her eyes."

On that day, with nerves dancing in my belly and all my dreams coming true with the wedding band snug up against my engagement ring, I realized the power of laughter in a family. My father had been teaching us all along, as he and my mom spent the 936 pennies of our childhoods. Through spontaneous water-gun battles in the house, to my dad's ridiculous jokes that never failed to bring a smile to our faces, we gained the life-giving education of laughter. Years later, with a family of my own, that education would prove itself priceless. I see it now in my boys' eyes when we step outside of the expected and surprise them with a joke or a silly antic. When a heavy moment is made a bit lighter with a bout of laughter, we're showing them how to redeem time, how to mark it fully with lasting memories and laugh-line making.

Because we've made laughter a priority in our home, I am keenly aware when it has escaped. When life grows busy and busy grows ugly—and laughter is pushed aside—life grows heavy. When it's missing, when we've shut it out—too busy to bask in its gift of life—a heavy burden settles on our household. Perhaps you have discovered the same. Everyone is a bit on edge. Not just Mom, not just Dad, but the children, also. In the absence of laughter, the thick of life settles over us. Laughter takes more than one person; it is a group activity, to be shared between souls enjoying each other. The enjoyment of each other is what we miss when we forget to laugh.

When a morning of rush turns into an afternoon of never-catching-up, which turns into an evening of too-tired-to-even-try, I find myself sitting on the floor with my boys. I tried the couch, but they beckon me to sit next to them on the carpet. I try not to notice the black dog hairs and cereal crumbs, evidence of a vacuum sitting neglected in the closet. When I sit there long enough, refusing to give in to accomplishing one more task that can wait, that's when I notice it. Depending on the day, it might take ten minutes, maybe five, perhaps not even one, until the tension unravels when at once I hear it—a giggle erupting quickly into a fully uncontrollable belly laugh. I follow the brilliant sound and not only hear it in my ears, but I see it in their eyes—their joy. Further, their enjoyment

> Laughter takes more than one person; it is a group activity, to be shared between souls enjoying each other.

of one another. And their enjoyment of me sitting there on the floor with them. Just sitting and being and soaking up their presence. My children seem to believe that laughter is an indispensable part of life, and they are right. Yet somehow between childhood and adulthood, we tend to give laughter a backseat. Life gets serious, and laughter seems trivial. My sons remind me every single day that laughter is not trivial—it is critical.

In those times when my soul is weary and my body aches with fatigue, I realize how badly I need it—their laughter to lift my soul out of the depths of life's frenzy. I go in search of it. No matter their own moods—serious, focused, or cranky—I dance. I jump. I make silly faces, because I am desperate for it—their laughter, which I have found to be one of the greatest medicines for my soul. My tired spirit has no more fight, and it does not want to fight. It yearns to embrace this refuge from the chaos, from the busy, from the disappointment, from the feelings of not being enough. Laughter offers this respite.

The greatest barrier to the growing of laugh lines is having a hard face. Those days when laughter is a miss from our home?

They are the days when my face is hard. Stern. Too focused on the heavy and too absent of the light. It never fails, in a moment when my face hurts from being held stern all day, and I relent, glance at my son, contort it to a silly display—he breaks with laughter. And I wonder where that laughter was all day. Did it hurt him to bottle it up, to have no release for this joy he was capable of but was given little opportunity to express? That is when I am reminded that I am their invitation for laughter, and they need to be extended that invitation every single day. It pains them to bottle it up, and it pains me to not receive their gift.

Maybe you have experienced this yourself: on those days when life is heavy and time is rushed and our days feel as though they've faded into unintentional territory. When we speak those lies of, *This day is no good. I've screwed up too bad. There is no redemption for the hurt of today.* And then, in one moment of deep grace, our child breaks into laughter and invites us to do the same. We behold the sheer power of it all; laughter can certainly turn a bad day around and fill our penny jars with meaningful moments of deep connection.

No matter how a day has unraveled itself, laughter gives us space to heal, to turn around, to return to a path of intentionality. Laughter offers us a respite in which to shake off the heaviness of the day. In its therapeutic fashion, it buffers our 936 weeks from heavy burden and gifts us with an ever-present reminder that this time was meant for enjoying one another. Can we let that soak in? That we have 936 weeks, if that, to enjoy one another side by side?

Can we sit on the floor for ten minutes, five minutes, or less than one—however long it takes for us to mingle our laughter together, watching it intertwine into a thread that will bind us together as a family, one to last beyond our penny jars?

That day as I sat as a brand-new bride next to her groom, my father had passed on a great responsibility. I stared at my mother, a table away, and I saw them, those faint lines my father spoke of. The gentle crevices marking my mother's face with years of enjoyment. I knew that day that my face was primed for those same lines, prepared ahead of time by nineteen years of watching my father make my mother laugh, and of me joining in that laughter, becoming a part of a family who enjoys each other.

My husband has faithfully kept his vows since that day, including the challenge that my father gave him. Not a day goes past when Grayson does not bring laughter to my heart, and in it I have seen the truth of Proverbs 17:22: "A cheerful heart is good medicine." Laughter has a beautiful way of keeping our bodies, our hearts, and our minds healthy. It melts away the stress of a day, and connects two spirits on an intimate level. It brings families together and knits together a strong sense of kinship between our children and us to last even beyond these 936 weeks.

I didn't know it as I sat at that table, but in two years I would cradle my first son in my arms, and that's when I would understand that laughter is a legacy. My father has spent his life making my mother laugh, and I, their daughter, am better for it. I am the benefactor. And as I would kiss my tiny son's soft forehead, I understood that he needed not only my arms, my milk, my attention, my kisses, and my prayers. He would need my laughter, because years from now, when he stands by his own wife and kisses the soft forehead of my grandchild, I need to know that my son is living a fuller life because he grew up in a home rich in laughter, and that he will pass on that legacy to his child.

Questions to Reflect On

- What words does your child use to describe nature, and how do those words reflect an innate knowledge of their Creator? What words do you use to describe nature, and what can those words teach your child about God?

- Whether you live in the city, country, or mountains, in what specific ways can you build more outdoor time into your weeks? Write down three specific ideas or outings and put them on the calendar!

• Is your family in the practice of enjoying each other through laughter? In what ways this week can you step outside of the expected and bring laughter to your child's soul?

-three-
Slowing
Time

We'll Trade Our Whole Life Away

I knew that something was terribly wrong the moment I opened the door of the microwave. I saw it, but could it really be? Yes, it could. There sat my mug of coffee, reheated for the fifth time that morning, sitting right on top of the electrical charger for our radio. Black, sticky, tar-like plastic was plastered against the inside wall of the microwave. And it stank. Bad. Like scorched plastic and electrical wreckage. I'm not sure if I was more upset about the electrical wreckage, or that I could no longer drink my coffee.

We were in the process of selling our home. Trying to keep a home presentable while living in it with three small children is nearly impossible. This morning was no different. We were scrambling to clean our house for two showings. The baby was refusing his morning nap, the boys were complaining about the green onions in their eggs, there were counters to be scrubbed, floors to be mopped, and dirty laundry to be stuffed into hiding places. In our haste, we began tossing stray belongings into drawers and baskets. It appeared as though my husband had turned the microwave into one of those hiding spots, for an electrical cord that needed to be stuffed somewhere at the last minute. And really, who could blame him? I mean, who doesn't look in the microwave before using it? Or at the very least, who doesn't notice a large black electrical device in the middle of the turning plate before setting their coffee mug on top of it?

Me. That's who.

With the baby bouncing on my hip, I lit a couple of candles and removed some fresh cookies from the oven. It was all I could do to battle the smells of dirty diapers and seared electrical cord emanating in the air. It is alarming what we can miss when we succumb to rush, because rush seems to promise fulfillment, reward, and purpose. But all it really does is steal from us what we'll long for ten years from now. If we are not careful, we will trade our whole life away in the name of speed and efficiency.

When I give in to the allure of haste, it's not only electrical cords in the microwave that go overlooked. It is also a frightened toddler, unsure of all the change pressing in around him, asking me to hold him. And a four-year-old after I've hushed him one too many times, breaking through my stress to whisper, "Mama, I just want to tell you that you're nice. And I think you're pretty." These moments are what life is made up of, and I miss so much of it when I refuse to slow down. Yet it is only when we slow down that we realize just how unnecessary rushing is in the first place. It ends up that rush is never worthwhile.

Perhaps I had never seen these things so clearly as when we were selling our house. In the chaos of showings and packing and working and raising babies and preparing for the biggest move of our life, rush lurked around every corner, threatening to steal away those moments that I so desperately wanted to hold on to. In the busyness of it all, our family was forgetting what was most important. We were forgetting to stop and enjoy the process. We were forgetting to sit and enjoy each other. Rush was hijacking our fun.

That morning, with potential buyers visiting our house, I found myself very grateful for a few hours to spend with my family without a plan or agenda. The frenzy of preparing for a house showing and accidentally cooking an electrical cord slowly became lesser matters as I shifted my mind to what was in front of me, and that was my family.

As my husband and I sat sipping coffee and taking our time to eat brunch, we found a much-needed respite from the hectic reality we'd created. It is those quiet respites that always offer us a glimpse into the things that really matter, a gentle reminder that the rush and bustle is never worth what we give up for it. That morning we made time to sit on park benches and swing our two-year-old "higher, higher!" We made time for watching our four-year-old scale new heights on the play set. We made time for feeling the breeze and memorizing how it tousled our infant's hair. We found time to think upon the One who created time and put us here to enjoy it. It ends up that time doesn't fly when you're having fun—rather, it slows, widens, breathes, and imprints itself on your history. Sometimes we need to just let time be what it wants to be instead of forcefully reshaping it into what we think it ought to look like. Time, after all, has a way of bringing beautiful moments right to us as we practice the art of paying attention.

> Time doesn't fly when you're having fun—rather, it slows, widens, breathes, and imprints itself on your history.

On that day, time wanted to tick slower, and so I let it. I can never stop it. None of us can. But we can slow it. We can weigh it down by paying full attention to the beauty that surrounds us. We can capture it with the making of memories. We can amplify time by spending it outdoors, where we come to know the Creator of trees and rivers and mountains and our babies and time itself. Yet all of those moments are stolen when we refuse to slow down. When we rush and force and push and work until we drop. And then we look back, and time is gone, along with the memories it could have held.

My husband has to constantly remind me of this. The truth is, I'm not very good at slowing down, but I am learning. And that is what matters. Every time we choose to take a step back and say no to the rush of life, we win. We become better trained and more adept at living a life that really matters, one in tune with the gifts of life that are often hidden among the chaos. We learn to prioritize relationships over tasks, and our children take note of these changes within us.

It is difficult, of course. After all, the dishes still need to be washed and the laundry folded. It is hard to slow down when there is so much to do. But what if 25 percent of the things we "have" to get done, don't actually need to be done? What if some of those extra tasks could be taken off our plates? What if the floor went a day without being swept? What if some of those extra activities and carpools could be taken out of our agenda, in the name of more time to be spent as a family? Slowing down is always a choice, and it always demands effort on the forefront. Sometimes it is these small changes that afford us all of that extra space to breathe that we have been longing for.

But what does this look like in the messiness of everyday life? In my home, it has meant that my husband helps with the housework so we can get it all done in a shorter amount of time. And when I say "all," let me point out that my "all" has changed. I have had to readjust my standards and my expectations. Our season of life is filled with sticky fingers, building blocks, and spilled bowls of cereal. But I only get this season once, and so I must accept the mess for what it is, reevaluate my ideas of how clean a home needs to be, and choose to spend less time doing and more time being present with my kids while I have them right here. If we are rushing around to get everything done, then we are bound to miss something. And most likely it will be our kids.

Depending on your circumstances, it might mean hiring some help around the house to free you up to truly be with your kids when you are home. Or maybe it looks like asking a friend to come over and help you tidy up while the kids have a playdate, and then swapping and tackling her home next week. We need to get creative when it comes to juggling life's tasks, and the balance of rest, work, and play. And sometimes we need to just set aside the work in the name of investing our time side by side with our child.

Twenty years from now, when I look back on my children growing up, I want to see myself sitting next to them. And so I must choose that now, even if the house is a little messier than I would like it to be. I think my children would agree.

● ● ● ●

One thing did not escape me about that crazy phase of our life while preparing to move. While we were wrapping plates in towels and taping cardboard boxes, I kept reminding myself that it will be over in a few months. I knew that the billowing waves of our schedule would begin to settle back into ripples. But in those few months of busy work, my little boys were going to grow quite a lot. And if I was so consumed with the busy, I'd miss what was right in front of me. And I knew I could never get that time back. I knew that in order to hold on to that time, to pack it full of life and cement it into memories, I had to say "No!" to rush. It's a declaration that all of us parents must make, if we are to nurture childhoods and foster legacies full of life. It's a commitment we must make time and time again whenever we notice the poison of rush infecting our days. We must say it again, and again, and again. *No, I will not rush. It's never worth it. They—they are worth it. My time, attention, and affection. And I can only give them these things when I refuse to rush. So that's just what we'll do. We'll stop trading our life away.*

We'll choose to slow down.

Boredom Blocks

I see it in late winter, when there is a promise of spring hovering on the horizon but snow dirtied from passing cars still litters the ditches outside of our home. Cold mornings lay winter's claim to its last weeks, and we are still shut inside, growing more antsy by the day. I try to fill mornings with activities: learning letters, modeling clay, building blocks, coloring—anything to keep our boys occupied. Yet each distraction keeps their hands and minds busy for fifteen minutes or so, before I instruct them through cleaning up their activity while I prepare another. It can be downright exhausting. It's not that these activities are bad—not at all. When done with a good dose of intentionality, they provide one-on-one time for my boys and me. They create space for us to connect and learn and discover together. This is especially important for my eldest. He thrives best when we spend undistracted time with him, engaged in activities right alongside of him. Where I find I go wrong is when I am constantly setting things up to keep him busy, while I run around in the background attending to my own busyness. He is not satisfied because I'm not involved, and I am not satisfied because I'm constantly distracted by his plea for a new activity, or for me to sit down and play with him. Neither of us is winning.

I'm discovering more each day the importance of setting aside my agenda and attuning my heart to his—cars, trucks, mud, and all. I'm trading in the dirty dishes and work assignments for these more lofty callings. It's easy for us parents, in the day-to-day humdrum routines, to overlook the importance of connecting with our children—really connecting. Through the simplest of gifts such as eye contact or questions such as, "Hey, what are you drawing? Can I see?" or "What's your new book about?" we can shift the whole of our relationship with our children. Choosing to enter into the interests and passions of someone near to us is one of the greatest ways we can show love, and we are afforded this opportunity with our children around every bend and corner of our day.

One of the richest, most rewarding ways I have found to make these connections with my children is to nurture an atmosphere of boredom in our home. I like to watch as it unfolds. It begins slowly, and not without friction. I spot the opportunity in their eyes, as their gaze moves from one wall of the room to the next. I can see their minds turning, *What do I do now?* The resistance comes when they ask to watch a show. I say no, and they push back. I remain firm, a smile hiding just below the surface, knowing we're about to make that turn and crest the hill of creativity. They realize now that I'm not going to cave, and I watch as they hunt the house for something to occupy their minds and hands. Some days they grab a cardboard box and some markers, and their minds are set on a voyage to the moon. Other days they fill their little arms with a teetering tower of books and settle into the couch, losing themselves within stories. Sometimes they grab for their shoes and go hunt down an adventure in the backyard. It's all kinds of wonderful to watch your child solve their own boredom through imagination, creation, and discovery. And the best soil for these things to blossom is a fertile ground of boredom.

> Choosing to enter into the interests and passions of someone near to us is one of the greatest ways we can show love.

For these things to grow, I've found that there are three important ingredients that must be tended to. First, I must make time to sit side by side with each child, entering into their interests and engaging in their activities. Second, I need to create an atmosphere of boredom, where the grandest of adventures find room to blossom. And third, I must mix the two of these—boredom and my engagement. I need to enter into their imaginative play, right alongside of them, so that we can embark on those adventures together. This third ingredient is where everything comes together. This is where I as a mother enter into my child's world. I don't try to coordinate it or control it, I just enter in and allow myself to become captivated by what captivates them. I may offer ideas, but for the most part, I am a visitor eager to explore this world, not change it. Of course, this necessitates that I myself become a little less uncomfortable with the idea of boredom. As adults, we are adept at curing boredom by filling our agendas and checking off tasks. Boredom bristles against our society, and often ourselves. And yet, our children need it, and so do we.

When we cease from trying to cure boredom, and instead encourage it and enter into it ourselves, this is when we can be sure that the pennies we are investing each week are marked by our presence. Together, we and our children can look back in twenty years and recall certain memories and adventures—treehouse forts and tents under the table and voyages to the moon. And as we look back, our children and we will see those memories in vivid clarity, because we were all there for them, sitting side by side.

These opportunities sit ready and waiting for us. I happened upon one on an ordinary afternoon when something rather magical took place. I slipped out of the toddler's room after setting him down for a nap. On the other side of his door, I found myself standing in an eerie silence. I peeked in on the other two boys, who had disappeared into their own room. There they sat, brothers and best friends, building block towers and losing themselves in an audiobook together. I poured a cup of hot tea, sat down between the two of them, and invited myself into their world.

In our six short years of parenthood, there have been a whole lot of things that my husband and I have not gotten right. This parenting thing? It is a whole lot of trial and error. Emphasis on the error. But one thing we have always counted a good decision was to welcome boredom in our home. Because boredom is often where the greatest possibilities are discovered.

In her book *More Than Happy: The Wisdom of Amish Parenting*, non-Amish yet Amish-enthused author Serena B. Miller explains one reason she believes Amish children possess such a surprising amount of patience.

> Amish parents don't appear to be concerned if their child is bored. . . . That is seldom true with Englisch (non-Amish) parents. We tend to worry if our children aren't well-stimulated and engaged in enjoyable or educational activities at all times. I watch loving parents scramble to create an almost constant stream of entertainment and activities for their children and I wonder if this is the wisest choice. If one never has to sit still and engage one's mind as a child, if one is constantly being entertained, when does personal creativity develop? When does patience kick in? When does one ever develop the ability to wait?[1]

On those mornings where I run back and forth between dishes, Play-Doh, laundry, crayons, writing projects, letter practice, reading the latest parenting book, and reading Dr. Seuss, I see myself as one of those loving parents scrambling to create an "almost constant stream of entertainment and activities." Yet while I am setting out all of these building blocks for my children to grow their skills, education, and days upon, I miss one of the most important building blocks for their childhood—boredom. Boredom is where they are forced to create, and where they begin to draw conclusions about life. It is where they are afforded room to grow without a forced path or prescription for that growth.

It's a question I'm asked on occasion: "Does it get easier?" It comes from parents of infants. I find myself hardly qualified to give an answer. And in fact, I find myself asking the very same question to mothers with children older than mine, those parents in the phase ahead of ours. "Does it get easier when they learn to entertain themselves?" I pick up a hint of desperation in my own voice. *When does that magical moment happen when I'm not constantly providing entertainment?* I believe that we as parents have gone astray when we buy into the misunderstanding that in order to spend our 936 weeks well, we must constantly fill our children's agenda with activities. In fact, I think that this is when we lose time. It gets buried in a myriad of activities and events. Rather, we can fill time with imaginative adventure, creative ingenuity, and problem solving—all by weighing down the clock with generous chunks of boredom.

Sometimes our children's minds must be led to a blank slate, which boredom often does. And that is exactly where we meet them, their hands ready for digging, reading, drawing, climbing, and creating memories that will last well beyond those pennies in that jar.

Derailed

They file in and out, these seasoned conductors with gray-flecked hair. Their hands bear testimony to years of hard work, yet gently they compose together these tiny mechanics of children's dreams. One gentleman, in particular, catches my attention with his bright, rainbow-striped suspenders. Each of the men interrupt their focused busywork just for a moment to acknowledge and offer a smile to my boys whizzing past, running as fast as their little legs can take them from one exhibit to the next.

The first time we happened upon this magical place will forever be etched into my memory. The day was drizzly and cold, not unlike my heart had been lately. The boys and I had ventured into the city in search of some coffee, fun, and perhaps a glimmer of hope. This new city was still so raw to me; we had been here for only a few weeks. Every street loomed with the unknown. Normally that would captivate me with a sense of adventure and exploration—today it only heightened my feelings of loneliness. We parked the car with no particular destination in mind and began to stroll our way through a string of attached buildings, sheltering ourselves from the less-than-inviting elements outside. I wrapped the blanket tighter around my three-month-old son. His car seat cradled him safely within the stroller, and I covered it with a canopy of nursing cloth, willing him to sleep.

We stopped by one building with bright colors and lights; there was a promise of fun. "I'm sorry," the kind woman at the front desk told us. "We are booked through the morning." Inside laid an arena of adventure for little hands to create masterpieces from markers, stickers, crayons, and paint. But we would not find our glimmer of hope here. Yet she did offer something. As she handed my son a bag of activities and crayons, she mentioned a model train exhibit. My eldest was two and a half at the time and enamored with anything and everything locomotive. In his perfect and innocent fashion, he referred to every single train as "My friend!" Perhaps if we could actually locate this little model train museum, we could breathe another day. It was worth a shot. We followed the woman's vague directions through a maze of buildings. Finally we stumbled our way into Union Station, aghast by its sheer size and beauty. I searched for signs to the exhibit, asked around, and followed pointed fingers. Hesitantly I opened a door to the outside, bracing myself against the cold air as it rushed to find respite for itself indoors. I stepped outside, guiding the stroller down a forlorn cement path. I pulled my hood tighter around my face, shielding myself from the icy drizzle, and tucked a blanket tightly around my eldest. The baby slept soundly in his car seat.

We followed that cement path with no sign or inclination as to whether we were headed in the right direction. But then I saw the door: a humble, unmarked entry offering refuge from the cold, and with it a little sign for the exhibit. My heart swelled with hope as I stepped inside. We wound our way through the hallway, and then—there it was. And it was no small thing at all. Before us laid exhibit after exhibit of magical model trains, all different sizes and styles, illuminated by lights overhead and underneath. It was whimsical. My son's eyes opened wide, aglow with the wonder of a young boy taking in something so great he could not comprehend the whole of it.

Now, a year after we first discovered this place, I sat watching those weathered conductors working amidst the whizzing by of my boys. I thought back to that first day we came here—that magical day when God gave us just a little hope, through a train station discovery, that perhaps this new city wasn't all bad. Perhaps we would survive another day. Perhaps He was carrying us through to something great.

Today we had begun with a different plan. I had pulled little boots onto tiny feet and zipped up coats under blueberry-stained chins, then strapped those boys safely into their car seats. I had an agenda. But as I backed the car out of the driveway, my little boy's voice chimed in from the back. "Mama . . . train station!" I turned back to smile at him, nodded in agreement, and turned the car in the direction of their train wonderland. I had made a plan, but today my son needed something other than my plan. He needed room for that plan to derail and point us in a different direction. He needed to see engines pull strong cars, wheels glide effortlessly along tracks, trains on voyage, and seasoned conductors delicately running the whole operation.

It's incredible, the glimpse we can glean into our child's heart when we are willing to allow our own plan and agenda to derail. When we are set so rigid in our schedule, routine, and plan that there is no place for deviation, we often miss some of life's best opportunities for connecting with our children. When was the last time you allowed a day to unravel at its own whims? When did you last leave an entire day open and ready for your children to fill it with their own ideas and interests?

When was the last time you allowed a day to unravel at its own whims?

We hold a great deal of power over the course of our children's day. Where we go, what they see, what they taste and witness and experience—much of this is left up to us as parents. But I wonder what we might communicate to our children if we were to ask them, "Hey, what do you want to do today? This morning is yours." Or if when our own agenda is interrupted, we would respond not with an attitude of inconvenience but one of kindness and creativity. What if we met the derailing of our day with an attitude of, "Well, why don't we go take a walk instead?" Or, "Why don't we pack a lunch and go sit in the park?" In doing so, we might just turn the disappointment of a day into a grand adventure. Perhaps it is this type of response that will teach our children about what's most important to us in how we shape our days.

This is another thing that has not come easily to me. I am an extremely driven and focused individual. For the most part, this is a good quality to have. However, it has its serious downfalls. When I have it in my mind that I am going to get a certain amount of work accomplished, it had better get done, or I am a mess just waiting to unravel. It is very difficult for me to switch my mind from work mode to play mode.

Dropping our agenda on a whim is not an easy thing to do. But it becomes easier when we plan for these interruptions, and even anticipate them. I plan my week out fairly rigidly, but I am learning to leave my agenda flexible enough to embrace a quick change of plans. For example, I might have Saturday afternoon slated for work or writing, but when Saturday arrives and it's sunny and seventy degrees, the family is itching to go spend the day at a stream. It's easier for me to say yes to play if I know I have Sunday as a backup plan for work. This, of course, requires that we have a certain amount of margin in our life. But that margin and flexibility may be the key to bringing more peace to our days.

It might mean sitting down with your spouse and looking over your current agenda and obligations. Perhaps some of them don't need to be on your plate right now, and your home and family would fare better without them. Cutting out some fluff from our agendas brings us more freedom to say yes to the derailing of our days and spontaneous memory-making adventures.

I have found that on those days when I let my little ones have a say in our agenda, I feel the most free. Unhindered by a stiff plan or my ideal of what the day should look like, I enter into what matters the most to my child. And on those days, I often rediscover what matters most to me. More and more I am learning to see those days not as my own plan derailed, but rather as divine, unexpected opportunities to create memories. Perhaps the derailing of our day is the best opportunity to recalibrate and refocus on tuning in to our children's hearts. If you ask me, that's a great agenda for a day.

A Hot Cup of Resentment

I heard the unmistakable crack of eggshell against the rim of a drinking glass. Rubbing my eyes, I tried to decipher whether or not I was still dreaming. I wasn't. I leapt out of bed and ran to the dining room table just in time to find our four-year-old concocting breakfast. One glass held gooey yolk and half a shell. There was an unopened egg hovering in his hand an inch from the second glass as he looked up at me. "Oh, Mom, I'm just making a snack." It was five thirty in the morning. As I set his Eggshell Special up on the counter to be taken care of later, I mumbled to him something about reading books, then I crawled back into bed. Our boys have always been decent sleepers, yet they, along with the natural seasons, seem to go through phases of early waking. We were deep in the muck of one of those phases, and I was one tired mama.

A couple of hours and a few cups of coffee later, I was sitting in our backyard watching our three boys as they covered themselves in mud and drank water from the hose. Our youngest guy, hardly a year old, toddled back and forth with his bottle of milk captured in a bug net slung over his shoulder.

As I sat under the sun's warmth and sipped coffee like nobody's business, I sensed an unwelcome resentfulness within my spirit. I was harboring a grudge, and it was directed at my own motherhood. I felt resentful over the sleep I was losing, and resentful of the little boy who was at its source. I was resentful of the coffee in the mug next to me, that it seemed entirely too weak to face the day ahead of us. I was resentful of this exhausting routine

75

that had become a bit too ho-hum for my liking. Mostly I was resenting myself. Why could I not pull myself together and enjoy this precious season of raising little ones, no matter the sleep deprivation and challenges? Here I was grasping at the pennies in those jars on my shelf, willing each one to *please, please just last a little bit longer.* My heart ached and raced under the reality of time passing. And yet, resentment was whittling away at that precious time.

The boys worked tirelessly on their latest construction mud pit. Every few minutes they would ask my opinion on where the twigs should be placed, or if they could turn on the hose to fill up their boy-made pond again. I took a sip of lukewarm coffee and glanced at the Bible lying flat across my lap, opened to Colossians 3:12: "As God's chosen people, holy and dearly loved, clothe yourselves with compassion, kindness, humility, gentleness and patience."

Compassion, kindness, humility—the words felt uncomfortable. I knew that I had been anything but kind, humble, and compassionate. The morning was young, and there had been far too many raised-voice moments. Reluctantly, I read on: "And over all these virtues put on love, which binds them all together in perfect unity" (Colossians 3:14).

Perfect harmony. Is that at all a possibility in a home with three children who still can't tie their shoes, who ask for something every two and a half minutes, and who quarrel over Matchbox cars? Harmony can seem terribly elusive when you're in the midst of raising kids.

The next line is the one that backed me into a corner: "Let the peace of Christ rule in your hearts, since as members of one body you were called to peace. And be thankful." *Called to peace?* As if to a vocation or a purpose or a mission? Called to let it rule in our hearts? Perhaps this is the piece that many of us are missing as we change diapers, check homework, chauffeur to soccer practice, and tackle those endless piles of laundry.

When was the last time you felt as if peace was at command in your heart? It had been quite some time for me, and I was beginning to think that I needed to reacquaint myself with this promise of God—for the sake of my motherhood and family. I was beginning to see an inseparable correlation between peace and how we spend our time. Perhaps peace was a key player in helping us to slow the time, to take notice of our days and weigh them down with the things that matter most.

Rather than peace as my compass, I had been depending on my own ideas and agenda to keep our life hovering above a certain line of order. I thought that if I could just do more, if I could chip away at and perfect our agenda until it was a well-oiled machine, all while getting sufficient sleep, of course, then we would be golden. We'd reach our goals, pay off our debts, build a thriving business, raise kind children, run marathons, and attend church every Sunday. Everything would work. But then the toddler would wake during the night and cry for three hours straight. Or we would get to the end of the day of working and raising kids with nothing left in us to give and have half of that perfectly manicured to-do list left, many of its items yet to be crossed off. No, peace would not be a fruit of our productivity. In fact, peace would have little to do with our circumstances. If I was going to find peace, then I was going to need to come to peace with my season of motherhood.

> If I was going to find peace, then I was going to need to come to peace with my season of motherhood.

Our oldest son was entering this all-new phase of boyhood. His budding mind was working overtime to make sense of the world around him, and I was faced with the constant challenge of helping him decipher truth and reality and good and evil, along with how to ride a bike and write the ABCs. We still had two boys in diapers, and our sleep schedules were at the whim of the toddler. With three children who still needed help around the clock, I knew that rest and quiet would not be a natural part of our days. Instead, I was going to have to discover where peace was, and stock up for the journey.

I believe that one of the devil's strongest strategies against parents is to uproot their peace, to leave them confused, hurt, fearful, and overwhelmed. When we're most vulnerable, he injects the poisons of doubt, anxiety, hopelessness, discontent, resentment, and even despair. The mother who chooses to return to work begins to suffocate under guilt, feelings of judgment, and fear that she might be making a wrong choice. Or the mom who chooses to stay home struggles against loneliness, or perhaps disappointment over the monotony of her days. Or the father fights against fears that he won't make enough, or won't be present enough. Unrest waits around every corner, ready to unravel us. I began to see that the peace my heart was desperate for was a kind of peace that had become all but extinct in today's society. I needed a peace that was bigger than my to-do list, braver than my fears, and louder than my doubts. I needed a peace that would not only weather the storms, but calm them.

It sounds good, doesn't it? This kind of peace promises hope and life. But what if life's circumstances have left you doubting the reality of such a peace as this? The difficulties of raising children can leave us feeling as if this level of peace is a myth, or only for those with faith greater than ours. But this peace—the kind that challenges every last one of our doubts and holds the power to snuff out every fear—is for the weakest of us. It is for me, and it is for you. It is for those of us who are ready and willing and desperate for it. It is for those of us on this journey who feel at wit's end, and it is for today. But first, we need to dig deep into the depths of what, exactly, has been robbing us of this peace.

The Plan That Changed Everything

It would have been so easy. Convenient, even, which is rare in a house with three kids ages five and under. The toddler was napping. The older boys were contentedly constructing block houses together in their room. The house was quiet. *I could sit and answer a few emails.* "Mom, can you come build with us?" His question jolted me out of my thoughts, which were quickly spiraling into productivity mode. "I'd like to, buddy, but I need to finish up a little bit of work." "Okay," he replied, "maybe later." He turned and walked out of the kitchen, and immediately my mind went to that little list hanging over my desk. Not my to-do list, but in fact the very opposite. I thought of that one line written on it: "No work between 8 and noon." It was eleven—*their time.*

I poured another cup of coffee and walked over to my boy. "I changed my mind," I told him. "Can I build a house with you?" He smiled and jumped in the air, then rushed off ahead of me to his room. We sat there together, me and my boys, for quite some time. I found it hard, somewhat restless. But with each passing minute, I felt more at ease. There on that unswept floor with blocks and trucks and dust bunnies surrounding me, I was right where I was supposed to be. When we finished our grand construction, I set up their beanbags against the wall, grabbed a stack of books, and we settled in, a boy on each side. That is where peace resided, and on that day I had chosen it, guided by that little list pinned above my desk.

Peace is not arrived at on a whim or a wish. Yes, we can happen upon a tranquil sunset or stumble upon a serene moment of quiet on the rare occasion that all the children nap at the same time. But the thing about peace is that we must work for it. The pursuit can be an arduous one, requiring great attention and resolve. But it is well worth the chase. When we as parents are at peace, our children feel it, and they benefit from it. As James 3:18 says, "And the seed whose fruit is righteousness is sown in peace by those who make peace" (NASB). Our job as parents is to be peacemakers. We can make peace in our homes by first discovering a deep sense of peace for ourselves, the sort of peace that roots itself only in Christ himself.

> **Peace is not arrived at on a whim or a wish. . . . We must work at it.**

Proverbs explains, "Those who promote peace have joy" (12:20). Peace, for parents, does not come by chance. Instead, we must make a Peace Plan, a strategy to direct us to the most fulfilling life. It acts as a regular check-in for our hearts to make sure we are where we want to be. For me, before anything else, I had to do some uncomfortable digging and unearth what was eroding the peace in my spirit. I began with the two questions that would become the foundation of my Peace Plan.

What specifically was robbing me of peace right now? I call these my Peace Thieves. Those things that lurk on the fringes of our everyday, ready to stealthily attack and rob us of our calm and quiet before we are at all aware of what is happening. And then the second question: How specifically could I combat those Peace Thieves, and by doing so bring more peace into our days?

Right away I could place a finger on some of the things that had been uprooting my peace. The rush of our mornings was certainly one; the frenzied escapade that ensued as we ran around getting everyone ready and out the door in time. Perhaps it wasn't even necessary. What would it look like if we reevaluated our appointments and crossed half of them off the list?

I was beginning to get a picture of the sacrifice this Peace Plan would demand. Another big Peace Thief was my snooze button habit. I had always been a morning person, waking before the sun as early as my high school days. But with the birth of our third child, that habit had been left behind in the delivery room. Now most mornings began with children jumping on the bed and telling me it was time to make breakfast. I had no time to prepare my mind or heart for the day, no time to be filled up before I could pour myself out. Because I was not waking early, I was missing out on my one opportunity to greet the sunrise with a calm and quieted spirit. I was handing over the best time in my day to read, pray, or write—three things that I knew to be peace bearers in my life—and I was trading them for the pillow.

With a few of my personal Peace Thieves down on paper, I pivoted my thoughts toward what might soften the edges of our days. What had I always wanted to write on the canvas of our days that had dropped down to the bottom of the schedule, left unattended? These were the things I wanted more of—activities I knew would bring peace but had yet to be made a priority. They were the things my soul longed for more of, things like reading, writing letters to friends and family, taking walks, sitting by the river, playing with the boys on the floor, and hiking with my husband. Many of them were my favorite things. I was beginning to see how short our time is to ignore these things that fill us up.

I couldn't wait, not only out of my excitement to chase down peace, but because there really was no time to wait. If I was going to do this, if I was going to take time by the reins and tell it how I wanted to spend it in order to find peace, then I was going to have to do it now, before I handed over any more of our pennies to those Peace Thieves.

And so I began to write:

Early morning time alone—before the kids wake
Slow mornings at home, or at the park
No running unnecessary last-minute errands

Time alone on the trails
Reading time with the boys
Family hikes
No screens 8 a.m.–noon
Read a novel
Purposeful prayer

When I was finished, I pinned the list next to my desk, where I could revisit it often, using it as a navigational beacon for our days. And as that little list hung above my desk, it began to take effect. It began to shift our days toward more intentional, less reactive living. It began to give me peace.

A Peace Plan is not a to-do list. Rather, it often looks like a *do-not* list. When we name the things that we are *not* going to spend our time and energy on, only then are we free to pursue those things that bring us peace and purpose in life. A Peace Plan is a constant reminder to me of what my heart really desires and needs. It is a reflection of my highest values. It is a warning light when I'm slipping into distraction or losing sight of what matters most in my life. This guide lays out boundaries, ones that state we'll say no to too many scheduled activities and yes to more family picnics. It might look like saying no to cell phones at the dinner table and yes to bedtime stories before lights-out. It might mean no to TVs in bedrooms and yes to family dates on Saturday mornings. Maybe it looks like a little more grace for takeout after a particularly exhausting day.

A Peace Plan is not a to-do list. Rather, it often looks like a **do-not** list.

Perhaps it means saying no to working at the laptop after dinner and yes to a set screen-free time each evening. Maybe it looks like filtering your social media feeds, removing that which discourages or evokes fear, and replacing it with streams of encouragement. Maybe it is a no to opening that news article that you know will haunt you for days and yes to picking up your Bible. Perhaps it looks like fewer home projects and more naps. Less doing, more being. It might look like us stay-at-home moms setting down the dish towel or the broom or the TV remote or the cell phone and squeezing in a nap whenever we get a chance. Maybe it looks like a bubble bath after the kids go down.

A Peace Plan looks different from family to family. Our job is to craft, hone, adjust, and improve on our own. The first step is to ask ourselves a question: What is currently robbing me of peace? Only then, once we have identified those Peace Thieves, can we create a list of defense—our Peace Plan—to protect, guard, and give fuel to a life marked by peace. That is when we gain ground in this fight. If Satan has been employing the strategies of fear, angst, resentment, or insecurity in your heart, a Peace Plan will equip you with the weapons to fight back and reclaim the peace in Christ that is already yours. His promise is sure and steadfast: "Peace I leave with you; my peace I give you. I do not give to you as the world gives. Do not let your hearts be troubled and do not be afraid" (John 14:27).

I have noticed a direct correlation with my level of peace and how I spend the pennies in our jars. Peace weighs down time and grants it richer meaning. Peace allows us to sit, rest, and take in the best of these days. Peace says no to rushing and no to wasting. Peace takes the reins of time and gives us clarity on what it is we want out of these 936 weeks. Whatever it looks like, I know this for certain—if we do not plan for peace, it will elude us.

As parents we do a lot of planning. We plan for vacations and birthday parties. We plan for school fundraisers and college tuitions. We plan for playdates and summer camp. But what if we are missing a Peace Plan, one of the most important plans we can make? It might just be the plan that changes everything.

Chamomile Tea

"Hey, Mom, can you smile at me?" That question stopped me in my tracks. I had been busy, preoccupied, stressed, and distracted. Sound familiar? These crazy seasons of life seem to creep up without announcement, and one day we find ourselves where we never meant to be, hardly holding our heads above the waters of busyness and distraction. And our children's words serve as a lighthouse beacon, guiding us back to shores of refuge and purpose. The simple request of my son left me with my breath caught in my throat. Since when did my son have to request a smile from me? My mind had been in a million places—but not with him. And somewhere in the mess of it all, I had misplaced my smile, and he had taken notice.

Over the next few weeks he would repeat his request on several occasions, each time finding my spirit a little more unsettled. Our children's words serve as an unrefined and unedited reminder of what they need from us. It wasn't that I was not happy—not at all. It's just that sometimes our smile can get buried under the pressures of life. Leave it to my boy to notice the little things that are actually the really big things. Like when Mom's smile starts to fade.

It wasn't only his request that had me considering my priorities. In the rare moments when I would set our busy realities aside in favor of a book, I was reading *Hands Free Life* by Rachel Macy Stafford. In the book, Stafford speaks of "keeping track of life," a term her young daughter coined. Stafford explains it like this:

Keeping track of life is knowing you're on your true path toward fulfillment. It's being at peace with who you are and how you are living. It's placing your head on the pillow at night knowing you've connected with someone or something that made your heart come alive. It's investing in what really matters, understanding full well that managing life is the tendency but living life is the goal. . . . It is a conscious decision to focus on what really matters when a sea of insignificance tries to pull you away.[2]

That sounds like a wonderful way to spend our 936 pennies, if you ask me.

I knew the busyness of our family's current season was necessary. But I also knew that I could not allow what mattered most to take the back burner. I could not stop smiling for my boy. *Or for me.* I was determined to take back our days and redirect them toward significance. This is when my obsession with chamomile tea took root. In those instances when I felt the tension nagging at my shoulders—when stress was rising and my neck began to tighten—I would heat up some water, stir in a spoonful of honey, and submerge a bag of chamomile tea. I'd watch the steam swirl above my mug as it steeped, then sit to sip and savor a few moments of pause.

Before long, our middle boy, Ellis, began to notice my new habit, and he wanted to join in. One particular afternoon, as I sought to calm our day that was threatening to slip into chaos mode, I reached for a bag of tea. "Can I have tea, Mom?" I smiled at him and grabbed an extra mug and a bag of berry tea. I stirred some extra honey into his tea and cooled it down with some cold water before slipping a bright orange straw in and placing it onto the table next to mine. There we sat together, sipping our tea and talking of our day. And before I knew it, all of the tension in my neck had melted. With a simple cup of tea, we'd reclaimed control and pushed away any sign of chaos or stress or rush. We had redeemed time.

It has been practices such as these—sitting to savor a hot cup of tea, to read a few pages in a book, or to dig in the dirt with my boys—that have served as sacred pauses in our day. They act as transitions from activity to activity—a reminder between tasks and activities to stop and remember what all the work is for. A few minutes to ask ourselves, "Am I spending this day on things that truly matter?" These transitions have quickly become an anchor to our days. They're often the springboard for meaningful conversation, or an invitation to making memories among the green grass and rain puddles. These transitions are a way of giving myself permission to sit and play, to read and think, to rest and wonder, to refocus and reclaim.

> The One who made us, surely He knew our tendency to default to busyness—and He wants more for us.

Perhaps this was the heart behind God's ordinance of a sabbath rest. As the One who made us, surely He knew our tendency to default to busyness— and He wants more for us. I want more for my kids, too. I want more than pressured days and stress-filled schedules. I want more than demanding agendas and exhausted evenings. I want them to know rest, fully and thoroughly. I want them to understand that God made us to enjoy His creation, and to discover true fulfillment in Him—not in our work. I want them to know that "there remains, then, a Sabbath-rest for the people of God. . . . Let us, therefore, make every effort to enter that rest" (Hebrews 4:9–11). I want to show them exactly how it's done—through tea-sipping and hammock-swaying and time-taking.

I have come to believe that parenthood must always begin with rest. I read them in college and they would never escape me: the words of Watchman Nee, a leader in the indigenous church movement throughout China from 1903 to 1972. He wrote,

> In the creation God worked from the first to the sixth day and rested on the seventh. We may truthfully say that for those first six days

he was very busy. Then, the task he had set himself completed, he ceased to work. The seventh day became the sabbath of God; it was God's rest.

But what of Adam? Where did he stand in relation to that rest of God? Adam, we are told, was created on the sixth day. Clearly, then, he had no part in those first six days of work, for he came into being only at their end.

God's seventh day was, in fact, Adam's first.

Whereas God worked six days and then enjoyed his sabbath rest, Adam began his life with the sabbath; for God works before he rests, while man must first enter into God's rest, and then alone can he work.[3]

This idea of "make every effort," or to strive toward rest, seems paradoxical at first. Is striving not the very opposite of rest? But when we look deeper to the roots of the word *striving*, it gives the idea of an endeavor, of giving our due diligence toward a cause, and to study something. Striving, it ends up, looks a lot like chasing after rest by unearthing it from every piece of our day. We spot it and lay hold of it. We see the opportunity for a pocket of rest, and we don't allow it to escape us, because in order to do the work well, we must begin with rest.

These integral breaks throughout my day serve the same purpose as the ancient practice of sabbath—a time to stop, reflect, refocus, and rest. And that is exactly where I find strength to continue on. We must first enter into God's rest, and then we can get to work spending our 936 pennies in a lasting manner. Sometimes it's found in a cup of tea, and other times in a walk around the block. Maybe it's in the pages of a good book or in watching the sycamore leaves sway in the breeze. Whatever it be, find those things that signal transition—the stopping place between tasks on that to-do list: sabbath-rest moments available to us each and every day. We can't always toss that list out the window. Things need to get done. But we can string together those tasks with a thread of purpose, and mark them with meaning through the act of sacred pauses. After all, looking back in twenty years, it's not going to be the folded laundry piles and checked-off work tasks that we remember. It will be the steam dancing atop our mugs and smiles shared with a three-year-old over a cup of tea on an ordinary afternoon.

Tire Swings

For four months of my life, I collected a great span of memories as I read and journaled through Ann Voskamp's book, *One Thousand Gifts*. In her book, she invites readers along her own journey—the acceptance of a simple dare posed to her—to write down one thousand moments, one thousand things she was thankful for. This dare necessitated that she learned how to slow down time with attention; she had to hone the habit of paying attention—of noticing.

As I followed Ann's journey, I embarked on my own. I began noticing. I began searching for those moments for my own list. That list of one thousand moments—it changed me forever. Not only did it build me one thousand blessings stronger, but it taught me to dig deep and pick apart my life, to acknowledge what truly mattered, and to capture every precious thing in life that I could, simply by giving it recognition and naming it as significant.

I realized also during that time that this is the reason I write. When I write, I am always searching for not only a plot or a story, but all of the lessons it holds within. I hunt around every corner, looking thoroughly throughout each moment for significance. I write because it commits my memories not only to paper or blog, but also to my soul. It helps me to see myself, my family, my purpose, and my life with much greater clarity.

You can do the same, and you must, if you truly desire to expand the 936 weeks you have with your child, making them into something much greater, much bigger than what they may seem at first glance. Those pennies look so few and can seem quite limited.

Nine hundred and thirty-six weeks from birth until our children turn eighteen. But when we set our souls on slowing that time and expanding it by taking notice and appreciating the moments that make up those weeks, we do it. We expand time. Suddenly a jar of worn pennies transforms into a treasure chest of countless moments, all building on one another to form a childhood bound together by beauty and significance.

At first, slowing time and expanding it with your full attention might feel a bit unfamiliar. It might in the beginning look a lot like another task. It will most certainly take time and intentionality to slow your mind, your heart, your eyes, and your day. It is a practice that must be attended to with time and resolve. But before long, if you stick with this practice until it takes root as a habit, it will become second nature for you to take notice and give thanks. You'll become proficient in slowing time, and expanding it with attention and gratitude.

Begin this week by carrying a small notebook with you. Every single day, write down three things that catch your attention. At first, you might need to train yourself to see them, to seek them out. Anything that makes you smile or wonder or see your life or your children in a new light, write it down. Anything that helps you to see your child for who they truly are, record it in that journal. The way he licks his lips after eating ice cream. The crease in her forehead when she's focusing on mastering that cadence on her guitar. The way he watches the robins splashing through the puddles in the driveway. These moments are what time is made of, and when we notice them, we become more aware of time itself. Time becomes more. And in a society constantly feeling the pressure of too little time—that time flies so fast and we can't slow the clock—this habit of giving notice to the small moments becomes one of the biggest blessings we can give ourselves and our children. It is the gift of time itself.

As author Ann Kroeker writes,

> To live more fully during those years when my kids were young, I determined to slow down and practice *noticing*. Somewhere along

the line, I started to turn toward my children and look them in the eye, holding their gaze an extra beat or two. I reached out to touch the bark of a sycamore and dip my feet in the cool creek near my house. I literally stopped to smell roses and summersweet, hydrangea and honeysuckle. I began to pay attention to life instead of letting it slip through my fingers.[4]

• • • •

There is an evening from the summer our oldest son turned three that has woven itself into the very fabric of my being. That penny in our "spent" jar shines brightly—a reminder of time filled full. The day was less than ordinary—in fact, it had been a rough one. I remember yelling. I remember anger winning over love, and sharp words spoken. I don't remember the offense, or even if there was one; perhaps I had simply been inconvenienced. I don't recall whether we went to the park, how many loads of dishes I washed, or whether or not the boys napped. I don't even remember what day of the week it was, or the date. But I remember the bonfire. My husband lit it when he arrived home from work. The air was warm; it would have been humid if not for the slight and refreshing breeze whipping the curls playfully on top of my son's head.

The sky was slowly transforming into a perfect blue—the shade of a peacock's feather—as the sun began to make its descent beneath the horizon. The air grew chillier; I slipped fleece pullovers over little blond heads and returned to my chair next to the campfire. My husband joined me with s'more makings in hand. We watched fluffy white sugar turn to amber and bubble over flames, then tucked it between graham crackers and chocolate before handing our son his first ever s'more. His mouth, rimmed in white and brown goo, smiled back at us with pure delight. When he had finished his treat, he continued his busywork of picking bean pods from the garden, then rushed back to me almost too fast for his legs to carry him. Carefully he removed shiny beans from their pods and deposited them into a small bowl he was using to keep them safe. He asked me to hold the bowl; I counted it a privilege.

At one point, I looked up from the fire to realize that the sun had completed its descent. We had put our youngest to bed a half hour ago, his little body exhausted from play in the yard, but still my eldest held out, picking those beans and licking sticky lips. I rose from my chair next to the flames, climbed our stairs up the back deck, flipped on the back lights, and then relaxed in the tire swing; my son quickly joined me. His body was heavy sitting in my lap; I could tell fatigue was setting in. He lay there, his body limp upon my own, swaying on the swing in the dark of the night. And there we sat, I don't recall for how long, because the moment defied time—it expanded it. It could have been five minutes, ten, perhaps fifteen, but all I remember is him with me, swaying, taking in the night, and taking in him.

We get one chance at these 936 weeks. Many of us, myself included, have fallen prey to the lie that we're told as parents: *We can't control time. It will always go by too fast. We can't slow it down.* But we do have the power to control time, and we must—for the sake of our children and our relationship with them, in the name of legacy and memories and a childhood marked by love and laughter and meaning and grace.

We are not left alone to be whipped about like the wind, vulnerable to the uncomfortable and demanding pace of life around us. We have the final say in how quickly or how slowly we live our days. It's a gift that money can't buy, one hard to find in our society. But every single one of us can afford it because it is purchased with our attention. When we choose to slow down those days by entering fully into them, we give our children one of the greatest gifts we ever could—a penny jar rich in life fully lived.

Questions to Reflect On

- How can you say "No!" to rush this week? Amidst the particularly hectic seasons of life, how can you imprint those times into your family's history as meaningful?

• When was the last time you allowed your day to derail for your child? Consider blocking off a few hours in the next week and asking your child what they would like to do with that time.

• Take a look at your current agenda. What are one or two unnecessary obligations that, if removed, could allow for more margin for you and your family?

• What are some Peace Thieves in your current season, and what specific actions could combat them?

-four-
Speaking
of Time

Callous Words

"Mom, sometimes I just wish that I didn't have brothers."

I nearly spit out my coffee. They were the most callous words I had heard come out of his mouth in his young five years. Fortunately, they seemed to bounce off his brother, Ellison. At three years old, Ellis was more concerned with what was for lunch. But I knew that soon enough, words like these would sting deeply. We had to address the weight of words now, early on. One of my regular prayers for our boys is that they will remain best friends as they grow older. Their years together under our roof are too short and too important for words like these to drive a wedge between them.

My husband was driving, so I turned around in the passenger seat to look at our boy. I knew this conversation would require both thoughtful words as well as eye contact. "Why is that, buddy?" I stepped gently into the waters, trying not to create a large wake too soon. Zeke looked down to his lap, fiddling with a plastic truck between his hands.

"Sometimes Ellis is mean and yells at me. And Willy cries, and I don't like that."

"Well, yes," I tried not to disregard his reasoning. Willy was one thing; there's not a whole lot you can do about a teething fifteen-month-old. But Ellis, it was true. For all of his sweetness, he could flash a mean temper.

"But we're working on it. And how would you feel if you didn't have anyone to play with?" I tried to search his eyes, but they remained fixed on his truck as he offered a cold reply.

"Happy."

I pressed on. "How would you feel if you went to bed tonight and Ellison wasn't in your room with you?"

"Happy."

"How would you feel if you woke up tomorrow morning and Ellison wasn't here?" The question made my own heart ache within my chest, and I wondered if I was pressing too deep. The boy has a fragile spirit. But his answer was unwavering: "Happy."

"Okay." I turned back toward the dashboard with a sigh, uncertain of how to get through to him. But then I heard the choke back of tears. I turned, and his mouth hung wide open, the onset of sobs a certainty. This is when he lost it. His body began to tremble within his car seat as tears rolled down his cheeks. I reached back and squeezed his hand, holding it tight within mine. It was five minutes before we could calm him down enough to get a word in and guide him through the apology process with Ellis.

I knew that this day would come. When our boy would discover the weight of his own words. When he would happen upon one of the greatest strengths—and weaknesses—that he could ever have. He had stumbled upon what the author of Proverbs scripted years ago, that "the tongue has the power of life and death" (Proverbs 18:21). Today Zeke had chosen death. And I prayed that through our discussion and the necessary pain that his little heart had to feel over his choice, that next time he would wield this powerful weapon for life.

So much of raising children happens through day-to-day conversation, if only we'll recognize the moments of opportunity to speak truth into them. Sometimes those moments can look ugly. In fact, many of the lessons concerning our words and what we say are taught through apology, as I humble myself and tell them I am sorry for my own harsh, unthoughtful words.

I would find this out the hard way one evening, when our oldest was five years old.

The day had been good. Together we had sat side by side with colored pencils in hues spanning the rainbow, taking turns coloring spots on a painted turtle coloring page. We proudly displayed the finished page on the refrigerator, "Zeke and Mom" scribbled at the bottom in my boy's sweet, rookie handwriting. That afternoon we had read through a pile of books, and I had lain next to him on the couch, his hand nestled within mine. But then that evening, when everything was rushed and my body was weary and dinner needed to be made and his little brother grabbed those scissors, everything snapped—along with me.

I had been busy in the kitchen, rushing to get some food on the table, when I glanced over to see a pair of scissors in Willy's hands. Zeke sat across from him at the table and saw it at the same moment I did. He reached to grab the scissors out of Willy's hands. The blades were open and, although they were dull, I feared they might cut into Willy's plump toddler hand. I dropped the piece of cake I'd been nibbling on and dove toward Willy and Zeke.

"Zeke! Stop! Let it go, now!" I tore the scissors from Zeke's hands. "Stop it!" The demand was hard and sharp. Zeke held in his other hand the bag of art supplies where the scissors had come from. I snatched it from his grasp and threw the bag down hard onto the side table. It was completely unjustified. I looked at my boy, and the expression on my face felt uncomfortable and foreign. It felt mean. And as my boy looked back at me, his expression was completely foreign to me, too. He was stricken and shocked. His eyes held fear. He had never looked at me in this way, and in that moment I realized that I never, ever wanted him to look at me that way again.

Despite the good day we had, one outburst of anger could have unraveled it all. It frightens me to consider the same potential for our 936 weeks—that our words hold the power to shatter days, weeks, months, and even years of trust with our child. Later that night, after numerous apologies, prayer, and reassurance, I could not stop thinking over what had conspired. I kept picturing the fear in his eyes. I had shaken his foundation and security—two things that our children are in desperate, vital need of. In our words and our voice, our children find belonging.

In the strength of my words that evening—as negative as they were—I realized the power that they hold for good or for bad, for building up or corroding my child's spirit. I saw that my words are a chief vehicle in communicating to them that they are safe, loved, and secure—but that in a moment's time, with a few quick words, I can cause them to question those things. Over time, as those hurtful words build up, they erode our child's foundation and their trust in us.

Not only that, but our words help our children to navigate their own emotions and vocabulary. What they hear on our own tongue will shape how they themselves choose to communicate throughout the 936 weeks and beyond. How I manage my anger—or fail to manage it—speaks volumes to my children. Proverbs says, "A gentle answer turns away wrath, but a harsh word stirs up anger" (Proverbs 15:1). In this promise we find the key to and hope for speaking gracious words to our children. Our words and how we speak them hold the power to defend our children against anger within their own hearts.

> So much of the anger that rises within me as a parent is a result of feeling inconvenienced.

I have discovered that so much of the anger that rises within me as a parent is a result of feeling inconvenienced. It's anger that shows up when we fail to remember that having children is altogether inconvenient at times, and our selfishness surfaces, which oftentimes expresses itself in our words. When I feel as though my own expectations or plans have been interrupted, or my own desires have been hijacked, I have to constantly stop and ask myself this question: *Will I respond with grace, or will I react in impatient anger?*

I pray that I will choose words garnished in grace, and that I will steep myself in the forgiveness of God—and my children—on those days that I choose otherwise.

● ● ● ●

Our children hold within them an incredible ability to forgive. Unadulterated by the world and its harshness, kids have a certain grace within them. I have seen it time and time and time again— after misusing my words and wronging my sons, they are quick to offer forgiveness without condition. When they forgive us, we must also work to forgive ourselves. This changes, of course, as they grow older. Forgiveness from a teenager may be harder to come by than forgiveness from a three-year-old. It is our task as parents to protect, nurture, and encourage that sense of grace within a child. And yet, whether forgiveness is offered right away or not, our job is to humble ourselves before our children, confess our wrongs, and make things right to whatever degree we are able. However they respond, it will move them on a deep level and show them that we are still learning, too.

●   ●   ●   ●

Sometimes it is our failures in parenthood that reveal to us just how tightly our hearts are interwoven with the hearts of our children. They show us just how severely we can feel our child's pain—especially when that pain is inflicted by us. We know it at the outset, rubbing that first swollen belly with our baby nestled safely inside. This precious one that we can hardly wait to hold, caress, kiss—we know that we will hurt their tiny heart. Our actions, reactions, and words will leave scars. Our love is flawed. It is one of the hard truths of these 936 pennies—they are marked by the tarnish of our humanity. We can't understand the depth of the pain until we rock the broken child, wipe his salty tears, whisper apologies. With a slip of the tongue, we fall short of passing on to them the love of Christ.

However, there is hope. We have it within our grasp to set up a net of grace for our children and us to fall on when it happens— when words are spoken and cannot be taken back. It is this net that not only buffers the fall, but also helps us bounce back up again, finding our relationships with our children stronger than ever.

Although our words are often what our failures are made of, our words can also act as the threads that tie this net of grace beneath us and bind together the broken pieces of our relationship with our child. As Ephesians 4:29 tells us, "Do not let any unwholesome talk come out of your mouths, but only what is helpful for building others up according to their needs, that it may benefit those who listen." Our words hold this incredible power. Although we will certainly use them wrongly, we also have the opportunity and responsibility to speak words that will build our children up. It is a high calling but also an incredible privilege to gift our children with words of life, and to witness them flourishing because of them.

Our words are one thing we will give our children that will last beyond these 936 weeks; words hold the power to influence them for the rest of their days, and for generations. So let's give them a legacy of wisdom, kindness, and truth wrapped up in the words we pass on to them today.

This Is Who You Are

"Mama, I love you the bestest, and you are pretty."

The first time I heard those sentiments roll off his little lips, my whole heart melted. However, this was about the eleventh time he had told me this in the past hour. It was midday, and my afternoon coffee was losing its effect, leaving me ill-equipped for conversing with a five-year-old.

"Thanks, bud." My reply was halfhearted. But then he spoke again.

"Is that a good encourager to you?"

I smiled. "Yes, love, that's encouraging to me. You are a very good encourager." It was a term we had introduced him to a couple of months before. We had explained to him what it was to be an encourager, and he had run full speed ahead as if it were his life's calling. He began identifying himself as an encourager. He would offer a sweet sentiment, tell me I'm pretty, that he liked my necklace or that I was a fast runner, and then watch for my visible response. Would I smile into his eyes, or offer a quick and distracted "Thanks"? My heart told me early on that this was his experiment. He wanted to see just how this encouragement thing worked, and how I responded could fortify within his spirit a lifelong habit of encouraging. I dreaded to think of snuffing out this quality within him. No, I needed to fuel it, because this world could certainly use more encouragers—those who will build others up through the power of their words. I determined in my heart that our 936 weeks would be used to raise some up.

We teach our children what it looks like to encourage by being the ones to first encourage them. We can make kind words that build one another up a seamless, organic, automatic part of their day by making it a key ingredient to the culture of our home. Proverbs tells us, "The mouth of the righteous is a fountain of life" (10:11). And with Christ as our righteousness, we have this gift available to us.

One way we practice this in our own home is through certain phrases that we've sown into our everyday conversations. These phrases act as brick and mortar, constructing a strong sense of belonging and identity—one they can use as a defense against the harsh words they may encounter as they grow up. These phrases are neither forced nor robotic. They are nothing magical, but they are also nothing short of life-giving. They are phrases such as:

A simple "I love you" as you look into their eyes.

"I love that God made you special in this way _____."

"I'm proud of you because _____."

"I saw you do _____ today, and it made me so happy."

"I love who you are."

"I saw you conquer _____ today, and you did great!"

"I appreciate that you did _____ today."

"I'm sorry I did _____ today. Sometimes moms sin, too. Will you forgive me?"

These are the phrases that weave together chords of a tenacious identity within our child. They are not mere flattery because they must, at their heart, be thoughtful and true.

Choose a couple of these phrases to sprinkle throughout your conversations this week. Watch your child's response as you speak life into their spirits. Observe how their confidence grows and how the roots of your relationship gain new depth and strength. These are the words of life that build up and patch up what was once torn down. These are the words that ground your child in their identity as *loved, respected, and appreciated* for who they are.

These "identity" words and phrases are indispensable when it comes to investing our 936 weeks well. They act as a force of protection against all that assails our days; all that threatens our time with our child. These words draw out life and purpose and beauty from our 936 weeks. As you speak these words to your child, before you know it you'll begin to hear the very same kinds of words rolling off your child's tongue. They are contagious in nature, life-giving to both the hearer and the speaker. This is how we raise our children to be encouragers, to be speakers of life. This is how they curb anger and embrace words of kindness and truth. It all begins with them hearing these words spoken over them— straight into the deepest parts of them that make up their identity.

● ● ● ●

There are seasons in our parenting when finding these words will be a whole lot more difficult. When a child is acting rebellious or traveling down a road we would never wish for them, encouraging words will be much harder to come by, or even seem as though they might cause more harm. But we cannot give up. Instead, this is when we must dig deeper.

Oftentimes, a negative behavior can be traced back to a positive character trait. A good friend shared a story with me about her six-year-old son. She told me that her son is a born rule-follower. He goes so far as to make sure that everyone around him is follow-ing the rules, too. This quickly became an issue when he would push or hit his little sister when she would break the rules. This is what my friend said:

> For quite a while I was trying to manage this behavior and
> continuing to get frustrated about how to handle the hitting
> and the crying that would follow. Then I realized that my
> son's desire for justice and order and rightness was some-
> thing that God had placed in him to reflect His own image.

Speaking of Time

The way my son was handling it was very obviously wrong. Because of his sin he was acting out a warped reflection of the image that God had placed in him. But when I start to pay attention to how the image of God was being reflected by him, even in the midst of these struggles, I am able to help him replace the warped image with a more godly one.

Encouraging a character trait is not the same thing as encouraging a wrong behavior. We can tell them, "I don't appreciate how you handled that situation," or, "You are going to have to be disciplined, but I do appreciate the passion in your heart." It gets trickier, but the hard encouragement can often leave a much deeper impact in our child than the encouragement that comes easily.

Oftentimes, a negative behavior can be traced back to a positive character trait.

Identity words hold the power to influence our children not only right now, but also in twenty years when all of our pennies are spent. But there is one thing we must address before we can speak these identity words to our kids. We need to take a good look at our own identity and see if shame is hiding in the shadows.

I believe that one of Satan's strongest weapons against parents is shame. Shame is more than guilt felt over our actions. Shame defines how we see ourselves. It lurks in between the crevices of our days, waiting for the most opportune moment to pounce. Its goal is always to cast a shadow over our perceptions of ourselves and our role as a parent. *You are too harsh,* it says, or perhaps, *You will never forgive yourself for that.* Phrases it has fired at me have been, *Only a bad mom would make that kind of mistake, he could have gotten hurt,* and, *If your husband knew you spoke to the kids that way, he'd be appalled.*

Shame lays a finger on every doubt we have in ourselves as a parent, and elaborates on them. And one way it finds to do this is to take our words and make sure they leave a disdainful mark on who we are. Shame tells us our words will ruin us, or that they have already ruined our child. That said, one of our greatest defenses against shame is our words: to take the very thing that shame wants to use against us and wield it as a weapon of defense. Speaking kindly to and of ourselves, whether out loud or in the ongoing self-talk in our minds, has a powerful way of overturning shame's grip on us. Instead of saying, *I'll never forgive myself for saying that to her,* we can say, *Wow, I should not have said that. I had better apologize right now and make this right. Those words were a mistake, but I am not the mistake.* From turning our attention away from how we see ourselves, and instead onto the offense itself, we avoid tying that wrong to our identity. It is not simply about positive self-image, though. It is about believing that God made us the parent of our child for a reason, and He's given us the grace and power to carry on the task.

As author and shame researcher Brené Brown writes it in her book *Daring Greatly,* "Shame corrodes the very part of us that believes we can change and do better."[1] And God's Word tells us "there is now no condemnation for those who are in Christ Jesus" (Romans 8:1), and that "it is God who works in you to will and to act in order to fulfill his good purpose" (Philippians 2:13). We are wiped clean when Christ is in us. He has become our righteousness and has done away with any reason for shame. God sees us in Christ, wholly forgiven. And we need to see ourselves in the same light as we parent the children He has given to us. Not only has He wiped our slate clean, but He also equips us every step of the way in raising our children; each penny we spend, He has given us grace to spend it well.

It wasn't until I began really listening to my son's words, instead of shrugging them off, that I recognized the power within them. "I love you, and you are beautiful," he would tell me thirteen times throughout the day—*but he meant it every single time.* And one evening after a particularly exhausting day, after my husband had sent me out for some retail therapy, he called me on my cell phone. "Eryn, you're the most beautiful woman I know."

"That's a lie," I told him.

"No, it's not." I could hear it in his voice, the seriousness and finality of his words. And in words and tone, I found identity. It didn't matter what anyone else thought. To him, I am the most beautiful. And that is all that matters. This is the power we have in speaking into our children's identity now, throughout these eighteen years, before they go off to face the world. We can tell them exactly who they are to us. And in that security, they'll have what they need to know exactly who they are for the rest of their lives.

"We've Got This"

There is a sort of camaraderie found in shared experience; I have seen this power through raising kids. I experienced it firsthand one day after a morning at the park with our boys.

I felt the woman's eyes on us from inside her car, parked next to our own. She had just buckled in her granddaughter, then climbed into the driver's seat and started the engine. I hoisted our oldest boy's bike into the back of our SUV as Zeke and Ellis climbed into their car seats. Zeke clipped together his top buckles, then they waited. I filled Willy's bottle with water and placed it into his eager hands. Then I doled out snacks and water cups for the big guys and finished strapping them in. Returning to the back of the SUV, I grabbed our two bags, along with snack wrappers and plastic trucks that had fallen loose in the bottom of the stroller. I tossed them in the front seat, then lifted the massive double stroller into the back, maneuvering it like a Tetris piece next to my big guy's bike. Finally, everything and everyone in place, the woman rolled down her car window. "Do you run a daycare?" She was serious. And I was struck by not only her question, but by the fact that this was the first time I had ever been asked it.

"No." I laughed. "They're all mine."

"Well," she replied, "you're doing a great job."

I don't know if she knew it—perhaps she did in her own experience as a mom and grandmother—but her words were an invaluable gift to me. They carried me through that day, as well as many others when I was feeling defeated. *You are doing a great job*. Sometimes that is all we need to hear. Words like these offer us space to breathe, to step back and reconsider. As parents, we can quickly slip into negative self-talk. It is very easy in the day-to-day to succumb to feelings of failure, to wonder if we are doing a good job at raising our children. But when we feel most poured out and empty, we are in the perfect place to discover the gift that a few simple words can be.

I saw it again on a day when the hours had stretched long and my husband had texted to tell me he had to stay late at work. It was Monday. He rarely works on weekends, but he had worked the day before, and today would be an eleven-hour workday for him—and me. Zeke called over to me from the table, where he was busy constructing an elaborate off-road Play-Doh track for his toy cars. One of his trucks was in dire need of someone to pull him out of the "mud." His four-wheel-drive had failed, apparently. I had no drive left in me, either. "Not now, buddy."

I lay on the couch, head buried in the cushion. Dinner remained in ingredient form, stuffed in the fridge and waiting to be composed into something edible. Thoughts of takeout danced in my head. My phone dinged to signal another text message. I reached for it, doing my best to ignore the mountain of dirty dishes sitting piled across the other end of the counter.

"On my way down" read the text. I calculated the time of his drive; he'd be an hour. I had an hour to pull myself, the house, and dinner together. Only I doubted that I would do so.

"I am beat" I texted back.

Within a moment his reply appeared on my phone: *"Me too. We've got this, babe. You're a rock star!"*

In ten simple words, my entire day shifted. I closed my eyes and took a deep breath. Seven years had passed since we exchanged vows and slipped rings of gold over each other's fingers, and he still knew exactly what to say. He still knew how to lift my spirits and convince me I could keep going. I set my phone down and called my boys over to the couch. They hopped up next to me, setting down a pile of books. Over the next forty-five minutes, we devoured that pile. We lost ourselves in the stories and in each other's presence. Time no longer inched by at a grueling pace, begging for my husband to walk through the door. Instead, time filled. That hour became what it was meant to be all along. After we finished our final book, the boys returned to their off-road track and Matchbox cars. I loaded the dishwasher, grabbed the cutting board, seasoned the chicken, steamed the rice, and rinsed the green beans. All the while, my husband's words echoed in my mind: *We've got this.*

That evening—as well as that afternoon when the stranger rolled down her window to tell me I was doing a great job—were both life-changing exchanges to me. Not only did they change the course of my day and perspective, but they also taught me an important lesson about the gift that words can be.

I am much quicker these days to look for ways that I can change someone's day—my husband's, a friend's, or a stranger's. Whether it's buying the coffee for the woman behind me at the drive-thru or sending a quick note to a friend, that simple notion of "Hey, someone is thinking about you today" holds incredible power to alter a day, or even a life.

For us parents who feel as if we're trudging throughout the muck and mire of our most exhausted, washed-up days; when our body and soul and heart feel entirely expended and we don't know how we will keep on doing it all, gracious words are exactly the medicine we need. Which also tells me that those parents milling about on the fringes of our day—at church and school and playdates and parties—they're feeling the same way. And gracious words may be exactly what they need today, too. A quick, "Hey, you're doing a great job," or, "You've got this," or, "Excuse me, can I buy your coffee for you today?" in the café line—offering these types of gifts to the parents around us can be the best use of our day. Sometimes our words can pull them out of a bad day and into one where they know that someone is thinking of and caring for them.

The day that shifted with my husband's simple text, *"We've got this,"* had begun much different from how I felt on that couch. I had read the words that morning: "Gracious words are like a honeycomb, sweet to the soul and healing to the bones" (Proverbs 16:24). But the long hours and endless demands had washed that thought from my mind. Yet with my husband's simple gift of words, he reminded me of this truth. Gracious words are a balm to a hurting heart and hope for the weary parent. May we make it a point throughout these 936 weeks to be one who speaks these kinds of gift words to the weary parent standing beside us—whether it's our spouse or a stranger.

Questions to Reflect On

- If harsh words have crept into your vocabulary, have you sat down with your child and asked for their forgiveness? Have you accepted that forgiveness? Have you forgiven yourself?

- What are three life-giving phrases that you could begin working into the everyday conversations of your home? Write them down and post them on the fridge or in your journal.

- Are you in the habit of speaking harsh words to yourself? What phrases or Scripture could you replace those words with that focus not on failures, but on your identity in Christ and the grace He gives you for parenthood?

- Which fellow parent can you encourage today? Send them a quick note; it could shift their entire day.

-five-
Standing the
Test of Time

Depleted

The two boys were getting unruly. They fed off of each other's energy and excitement, no doubt heightened by the sugary cream rimming their little mouths. Their boots *pitter-pattered* after each other as they ran across the storefront. The little one let out squeals of excitement as his brother chased after him. Their volume level was quickly rising, but I didn't care. They weren't mine, after all.

The boys belonged to the couple sitting a table away from us.

"How old are they?" I nodded to the boys with a smile. Their mother caught her eldest son by the hand to keep him from sprinting away to the other side of the shop. She slipped his hand into his coat sleeve.

"Two and four," she replied.

I smiled at her again. "I thought so. Ours are about the same." In my words I found myself grateful for friends watching our boys that night so my husband and I could enjoy a few hours out alone. The father grabbed the youngest and hoisted him up into his arms, only to reposition and catch him as he flailed to escape back to the floor.

"Ice cream always *seems* like a good idea," my husband commented with a knowing smile. Without missing a beat, the father replied, "Yeah, *they* seemed like a good idea, too," as he nodded toward the boys. There was humor in his voice, but I also heard exasperation, the voice of a weary father. And haven't we all been in his shoes?

Have we not all experienced that bone-weary exhaustion, the kind that seeps into our deepest parts? We only have so much to give, and some days demand more than we have.

Several friends of mine who have crossed that beautiful threshold of no longer having children in diapers look back on those years and explain, "I really have no idea how we got through it. We just did. I look back and those years are a blur." Maybe you have felt it, these years of raising kids too young to tie their own shoes or fix their own snacks. Whether you are in that season now or looking back on it, the days can seem a blur. The constant demands leave us empty, exhausted, and completely poured out by night's end. And then someone needs another bedtime story or cup of water.

Depleted and defeated, you may have wondered just how to press on. I can only imagine how much deeper these emotions run for a single parent. Whether we are changing diapers and kissing owies, helping with homework and soothing broken hearts, or handing over car keys with desperate prayers for safety, this parenting thing is not for the faint of heart. And yet some days, we feel just that—faint. Weak, weary, tried, and taxed.

This hit me particularly hard one day as I was thinking about Jesus and His disciples on the day they fed thousands of men, women, and children. They hadn't been planning on catering a large feast that day. They hadn't been planning on spending that day with anyone, let alone thousands of people hungry for bread and a dose of truth. The disciples were on their way to the mountains for some well-deserved rest. Finally, after days of travel and ministry, the time for respite had come. The anticipation for a nap was palpable. You know the feeling, I'm sure. Upon hearing of Jesus and the disciples' intent and direction, a multitude ran ahead of them, waiting eagerly for their arrival. And Jesus, upon seeing them, had compassion for their need. He bypassed His time of rest and sought at once to meet the needs of the people.

It was this picture that immediately brought to mind my own response to my children's needs in recent days. I pictured myself the week before, trying to snag a nap on the couch while the boys napped. Our oldest had come to give me another hug and kiss, pulling me out of my near-sleep state. I snapped at him, told him I had been sleeping, and sent him back to his room. I wondered now, looking back on that moment, how many opportunities for compassion I had passed up because of my own selfishness.

To be honest, I have struggled with this piece of Scripture telling about the crowds seemingly interrupting the disciples' need to get away and rest. Doesn't Jesus tell us that there is a holy rest for the people of God? Does He not call all who are weary and heavy-laden to cast their burdens upon Him? He does. And His presence is the sweetest place of rest we can ever discover. Yet sometimes it is the very service He calls us to—those precious opportunities for compassion—that usher us into His greatest rest. And perhaps the only obstacle to our entering into that rest is how we respond in a moment of inconvenience, whether or not we choose compassion.

When my children come to me for yet another snack, will I sigh with exasperation, or show compassion and meet them in their need for nourishment? When they come to me for assurance in a hug, will I brush them away, or meet them with kindness? When they're looking for a smile or laugh, will my heart hold compassion for their need of connection? And when I feel absolutely depleted at the day's end, anticipating some time for rest and to be alone, will I show compassion when my little one yells from his bedroom, asking for one more bedtime prayer? How we respond in a moment of exhausted inconvenience will speak multitudes to our children about the importance of compassion.

This depth of compassion is only within reach through the Holy Spirit's power within us as we lean hard into the promises of Scripture, promises like this:

> But he said to me, "My grace is sufficient for you, for my power is made perfect in weakness." Therefore I will boast all the more

gladly about my weaknesses, so that Christ's power may rest on me.

2 Corinthians 12:9

Jesus does not say that *your* power will be made perfect. He is not interested in increasing our strength, except through His own strength increasing within us. He says *my* power is made perfect (or *executed*, or *accomplished*, in the Greek roots of the word). Our weakness, our insufficiency, our exhaustion opens wide the door for Christ to accomplish His power within us. And this is the only way for us to choose compassion over convenience.

I believe that this place of compassionate service—depending on Jesus for strength to serve—is where we will discover the sweetest, most holy kind of rest, the kind of rest that will rejuvenate us for more than just today, but will carry us through every one of these 936 weeks.

"How Did We Do It?"

Excitement hovered in the air. A crowd of women were gathered in a side room of our church to celebrate the homecoming of a precious little boy from Ethiopia. For two years our entire church had prayed hard for papers to be signed, stamps to be pressed, organizations to do their jobs, and this boy to know a family of his own.

My own son, only three weeks old, slept soundly in his car seat next to me.

"It's amazing, you know . . ." a friend of mine said from the next seat over. Her daughter had recently celebrated her first birthday. "How they turn a year old, and you look back to when they were this tiny"—she motioned to my son all of five small pounds—"and you just ask yourself, 'How did I do it?'"

I knew exactly what she meant. The evening before had been marked by hungry newborn cries, a toddler fitful and afraid of thunder echoing across the sky, and a tornado siren that ushered all of us out of bed and down to the basement in the midnight hours.

I knew exactly what my friend was saying that afternoon at the adoption party as I sat sipping on my iced coffee as if it were a life source. I thought of our friend who we were celebrating that day, and the arduous journey she, her husband, and children had endured over the past two years to bring their precious boy home. Their adoption had been wrought with disappointment, fear, uncertainty, and heartache—yet here we all were, tears in our eyes, as we watched the video of his homecoming.

As we sat together watching photos and video telling the story of their journey, we all witnessed as a chocolate brown face with deep-brown saucer eyes stared back. As the photos progressed, this little boy transformed from a fearful babe to a toddler confident in the newfound love of his family. I was certain my dear friend, looking back at photos from the beginning of their journey, was asking herself now, "How did we do it?"

All of us, no matter how different the details that make up our stories, step out of a season only to look back and wonder, *How did we do it?*

And here is the simple answer: *we* didn't. God did. I count it all grace when I come to the end of a day and look back on the hours and see traces of God's patience and love woven throughout them. On the other end, looking back, this is when I see that His grace is enough to cover a multitude of my wrongs, my screw-ups, my mistakes and shortcomings, enough to cover a day with His goodness, and to name that day *good.*

Our days have been written down in a book by our Creator, who crafted us to enjoy Him and the journey He's given us. And He has promised us that His burden is light. "Come to me, all who labor and are heavy laden . . ."

Heavy laden. Burdened. Encumbered. Hampered. Fraught. Oppressed and weighed down. I know of no parent who has not felt this way. Jesus continues, "and I will give you rest. Take my yoke upon you, and learn from me, for I am gentle and lowly in heart, and you will find rest for your souls. For my yoke is easy, and my burden is light" (Matthew 11:28–30 ESV).

There is rest to be found for the weary souls of parents who feel like throwing in the towel. There is peace for those of us who at the end of each evening feel like we can't lift another finger, can't take another step, can't do another day. His promises are big enough for those of us still in the *How are we going to do this?* season.

I wondered about this passage for a long while. It seemed incomplete to me. I saw promise, hope even—but I didn't see the *how.* When God calls us to something so great, so magnificent, so holy, and so completely depleting as raising the children He's given us, how could it ever be *easy*, *light*, or *restful*? Is it easy when I've already used up all my patience reserve before nine in the morning, and then the toddler throws a tantrum? Is it easy when my son begins showing behavioral issues and I have no idea where to turn? Is it easy when my husband and I are not on the same page with how to discipline? Is it easy when we have to decide the best route of schooling for our children? Is it easy when the time comes to finally decide do we have another, or are we done?

Nothing about this is easy.

Yet that promise—I cannot dismiss it. And then one day I see it. The truth of His Word winds its way around my heart, resuscitating the parts of me that felt as though they had died of exhaustion. This is it, I realize; this is how God makes His yoke light, this is how He makes this calling on our lives attainable: "His divine power has given us everything we need for a godly life" (2 Peter 1:3).

> When God calls us to something so great . . . and so completely depleting as raising the children He's given us, how could it ever be easy, light, or restful?

God gives us everything for life and godliness—all that we need in the day-to-day dish-washing, carpool-driving, discipline-giving, moral-teaching, laundry-folding business of raising children. All that He has called us to He has enabled and equipped us for. That is the life-giving promise of a light load.

He never looks away, never steps away for a break, and never comes up short.

God is right there waiting for us to hand over the load and allow Him to do the heavy lifting. And not only for the overwhelming pieces to our days—He cares deeply about the tiniest of details, too. Just like at the wedding of Cana, when Jesus' mother came to Him with a great concern that to us seems rather minor: there was no more wine. Back in those days, a wedding celebration would last for days. And to run out of wine this early on would be a terrible embarrassment for the bride and groom. Mary came and presented her simple problem: *There is not enough.* Maybe you feel the same today. *There is not enough energy. There is not enough money. There is not enough help. There is not enough time.* Jesus beckons us to come to Him with our *not enough*s. Whether they seem like big needs or small—He cares. Jesus looked into the details of the bride and groom's life, and He cared. He performed His first miracle—not a healing or a resurrection, but the smallest of provision that in essence said, *This matters to me because I see that it matters to you.*

Jesus says the same today about the most minute details of our lives. When the week has been long and you feel you just cannot keep going, and then the baby gets sick or the car breaks down or the bills stack high—none of it goes unseen by Him. And if it is heavy on our hearts, then it matters to His. He looks down into the tangle of those details and gently reminds us that He has granted to us all things pertaining to life and godliness. As we're lugging around this sack of worries and burdens and fears on our shoulders, He's waiting patiently to grab them all and gently lift them off our shoulders. He's standing by to lighten our loads.

• ◦ • ◦

One day when our pennies are all spent, I know I will look back and wonder, *How did we do it?* My prayer then will be that when I see another mom, one still in the days of her penny spending and time counting—one still asking, "How are we going to do this?"—that I'll stop to look her in the eyes and assure her, *We don't.* God does. By His grace and His love and His mercy and His provision, and that small, steady voice of His spirit reminding us, *I am enough when you are not.*

They are the words I need to hear today, and every day, really. I'm sure you could use them today, as well. When we are questioning how we'll ever spend these pennies to their fullest potential, or even how we'll muster the energy to make it another day, the answer is always, *But God.* But God in His mercy will provide.

But God will come through. But God will make a way. But God is more than enough. For He is the one who "gives strength to the weary and increases the power of the weak" (Isaiah 40:29).

When we're not yet to "How did we do it?" but we're still in the midst of "How *will* we do this?" we need to remember that "those who hope in the Lord will renew their strength. They will soar on wings like eagles; they will run and not grow weary, they will walk and not be faint" (Isaiah 40:31). We wait, resting confidently in His promises and provision, and we watch for the *But God* moments to carry us through to tomorrow. Then, when we spend that last penny and peer into the empty jar, we'll know exactly how we did it.

Chisel

A gracious breeze travels from room to room through the open windows of our home. It's been raining for days, and now this perfect, sunny, warm Memorial Day morning reminds me that in the eye of a storm there is rest to be found—solitude. I hear their little voices carry through the yard, bouncing off green grass and sycamore trees, their excited chatter creating a melody with the birds' chipper singing—a praise song to a creative Maker. The oldest one runs across the yard at top speed, his face lit with wonder. "Daddy! Daddy!" he calls. He reaches the back door and unfolds dirt-stained fingers from the treasure within his palm—two bright red, plump strawberries from the garden. "Daddy! The strawberries are ready!" His excitement is overwhelming. He's been waiting for this—for those shriveled brown stems from last year to move aside and make way for fresh green ones, for the leaves that protruded from those stems to produce those delicate white flowers. Finally last week the berries appeared, hard and white and altogether not ready, yet altogether promising hope. Today was the morning for his discovery, and now those two wonder-filled boys tiptoe through that tiny strawberry patch as their daddy points out which ones are ready for the picking, and then they all retreat to the porch to devour their treasures.

My head hurts as I watch from the kitchen. Two nights in a row of our newborn boy waking every hour of the night to feed—it has left me fuzzy-headed and body-aching. Soul-aching, also—for rest, for creativity, and to feel human again. Some mornings I wake up feeling very ill-prepared to care for three young boys. They smile and munch. I search for my own discovery and respite. I reheat my mug of coffee for the third time. I hear those little voices quiet as berries fill anxious mouths. I walk past that wall in our house, the one with the shelf with those jars full of promise and challenge.

Today is Monday. I always plan on depositing these pennies each Sunday—yet every week I put it off. I've put it off for weeks at a time, only to deposit three pennies from each jar to make up for my reluctance to do it earlier. I tell myself it's laziness or forgetfulness, but in my heart I know better. I put it off for the same reason many of my blog readers tell me they could never set up these jars in the first place—it hurts too much.

It is too hard to visibly see those weeks being spent.

I stop, set my coffee next to the glass masons, and unscrew three lids. I take one penny from each of their jars and deposit them into the new jars. Another penny spent for each of them—another week. And I see it now—that these pennies filling these jars are not only theirs. *They are mine.* Those 936 pennies not only represent the time lapsing from their birth to their flying from the nest—but they represent 936 weeks of my own life. This adds to the difficulty of the task. As I place each penny into its "spent" jar, I think back through seven days. Seven days spent investing in little souls—and also investing in my own. Each week, each day—every moment I am entrusted to love, nurture, and grow my children—all of that time is also the time I am allotted to grow my own soul through the nurturing of them.

These pennies filling these jars are not only theirs. They are mine.

That morning I had woken weary and not ready for a new day. My husband got up with the older boys, leaving me to catch whatever scraps of sleep I could after another long night. The boys had crept into my room. "Good morning, Mama!" They jumped onto the covers and cuddled up beside me. "Good morning, Weyland!" They leaned in to kiss their new baby brother. My heart melted. My head hurt. I wanted to cherish the beauty of the moment, but more than that I wanted sleep. At breakfast I spoke sharply—telling them to hurry and finish their breakfast, to stop throwing food, to listen and obey. They bubbled over with excitement for a new day—one I'm not ready for yet.

I thought through these things as I deposited the pennies, of all of their beauty and excitement and discovery—and of all the ways I was challenged by those very things this week. Those pennies are not just shaping them, they are also shaping me.

The Bible tells us that children are a blessing. Sometimes blessings come in disguise. I now see it—that the blessing moments are not only wrapped up in the sweet cuddles, story times, "I love you's," or for mornings when everyone gets along and there is no bickering to be heard about who's toy belongs to whom. No, the blessings are also buried deep in the trenches—in the groggy mornings, in the guilt-ridden moments after we yell hard and sharp, in the pain-stricken faces of our children when their feelings are hurt by a friend, in the fearful evenings when they don't come home by curfew, in the uncertainties surrounding so many decisions we make with these 936 pennies—these all hold potential for blessing, because they shape us into who God wants us to be. They are His tools to hone and craft and chisel away all that is not of Him or His plan.

I asked the readers of my blog what has surprised them the most about motherhood, and I loved my friend Gretchen's response. She said, "It's a daily dose of the gospel. How God uses it to refine me. How the trials that He brings me through with my kids are as much a learning process for me and my own sinfulness and need for a heavenly Father to guide, protect, and love me. Every time I lecture my kids, God's tapping my shoulder and saying . . . 'Sound familiar?'"

My friend Hannah pointed out to me that being "chiseled" through parenthood is the best way to communicate the gospel to our children. She told me: "When I can be transparent about the work He's doing in me, it helps my children to know that He will work in them, too."

God uses these precious little ones who drive us crazy and challenge us hard—He uses them to show us himself and what He desires of us. Every one of these pennies is a grand opportunity for us as parents to be shaped and chiseled. And now as I deposit those pennies, I not only think back on how each week has shaped my precious children, but also how they have shaped me.

Questions to Reflect On

- Are you in the midst of a "How are we going to do this?" season? Look back over the past year and write down five specific ways God has come alongside of you and proven His faithfulness.

- What are your "not enoughs" today? Do you feel like there is not enough time? Not enough patience? Not enough kind words? Not enough energy? Lay these at the feet of Jesus and rest confidently knowing that He is enough.

- How might God be using your current season of parenthood to chisel you? What challenges is He using to bring you into a deeper dependence on Him?

-six-

A Perspective
on Time

Out of Control

The paper crinkled beneath my frail body with every slight move I made. I winced and felt the warmth of both a tear sliding down my cheek and the trickle of blood traveling down my arm. I could feel my father's eyes on me. They were full of concern, as had been the case lately. I stared straight at the ceiling, willing this part to be over. The tourniquet pinched at my skin. Songs from my favorite music group hovered in that sterile room, playing from the portable CD player my dad had brought with us for the day. I took in the acoustics and words of "Blessed Be the Name of the Lord." The nurse taps on the needle, adjusts its angle. My dad tells me to recite the alphabet backwards, and my mind immediately set itself to the challenge. Anything to not think about the warmth of that blood on my skin. The nurse apologizes again for the discomfort before leaving the room.

My dad will sit there in that cheap hospital chair for the next three hours, praying with me and telling me jokes as nurses come and go to draw blood. He will be by my side also in the weeks, months, and years to come as we learn the strings of my new diagnosis. He'll be by my side through each of these appointments, and after, as we create a tradition of stopping at our favorite Chinese restaurant for lunch together following each doctor visit. He'll send letters and emails and faxes back and forth between my doctors, letters that I will read years later, only then understanding the depth of his involvement in my treatment. He will sit beside me in the car, driving me late to school on the days when I just

131

can't muster the energy to get to the bus on time. He'll pick me up early on the days when I'm too dizzy to sit through class. When I travel to new continents in high school, he'll send instructions ahead of me to the adults on the trip. He'll pack my medications carefully, splitting them into two bags, just in case one gets lost. He'll make sure that I have multiple emergency injection kits, and that my emergency helicopter evacuation insurance is up to date, just in case. He'll be by my side as he trains me in how to avoid and manage stress, the nemesis of my disease. He won't leave my side. He couldn't control this disease that infiltrated my body, but he can offer me the security and hope that I would need as a young woman facing an uncertain future.

When the doctor first told us of my positive results—"Yes, she does have Addison's Disease"—our family had no significant medical history. I had been a healthy child up until recent months, when weight loss, fatigue, and dizziness had left dark circles under my youthful eyes. And yet here we were, dropped into a whirlwind of medical tests and terminology.

The doctor explained, as well as he could, the details of this relatively obscure disease. Before its discovery in 1849 by Dr. Thomas Addison, the disease was an unknown killer, a certain death sentence for those suffering. Now, however, my doctor explained that I would live on synthetic hormone replacements for the rest of my life. My adrenal glands no longer functioned, he explained. My immune system had confused the glands as a foreign object and attacked them, all without our knowledge, until they lost all life. My body had turned on me. Stress, we learned quickly, is my greatest nemesis. Adrenal glands act as one's chief defense against inward and outward stress. With mine out of commission, stress was free to have its way with my body, and in extreme cases, could send me into a coma that, left untreated, would claim my life. The shock of it all was too much for my fourteen-year-old self to truly comprehend. I sat quietly next to my parents as they nodded and asked questions, and we all tried to wrap our minds around what this meant for my life.

Yet through each new and unfamiliar step, my dad and my mom stood as my firm rocks. Only years later as a parent myself would I begin to understand how difficult it must have been to stand by and fake bravery, muster faith, and pray fiercely for their little girl in the face of this disease the doctors knew little about. Only now, years later with babies of my own, can I glimpse the fortitude in their spirits as they took on this thing that they could not control, and did the very best they could with it. In the unknowns, they offered me security. In the fear, they showed me bravery. In the questions, they offered me hope. And in so doing, they offered me life. They handed me the very tools I would need as I navigated my new world. With a disease that often dramatically lowers one's quality of life, they gave my spirit everything I would need for chasing after a full life. And so I did.

Years later, when I would birth babies the doctors didn't know if I could have, take up running long distances, start my own businesses, and enter my writing career, I can look back and see that every endeavor I have taken on with my broken body has a little bit of my parents in it. Every pursuit that took bravery, careful training, and sheer will, I can trace back to their gifts to me during those first years after my diagnosis. When they could have crumpled in fear at the face of this illness and its potential, instead they chose to do their very best in setting me up to beat it. And now, as I watch my boys run and play and climb and venture, whatever uncontrollable circumstances await us in the future, I know what is in my control. I can offer them hope, bravery, faith, and strength in the face of whatever comes against us. And I know firsthand how those gifts can help them beat the odds. This is one of the great tasks that we are given as parents, a part of our calling: to stand bravely and battle against the swarm of fears that threaten to engulf us around every bend.

• • • •

The first time you see that positive indication in the timing window of that little plastic stick, your heart swells with a thousand different emotions—they can vary greatly, depending on if the confirmation was expected, anticipated, or sheer surprise. It was only our first month trying to conceive, and I had convinced myself that our efforts had been fruitless. Yet there it was, that ever-so-faint second pink line. I was going to have a child! Or was I?

Included in my overwhelming emotions was an overbearing fear. I remember at five weeks along in our pregnancy being absolutely convinced that we would lose this child, that he would not come to be, that I would never caress his soft, brand-new skin. I had read too many books, too many articles, too many statistics of lost babies. The fear was immense, and it was conceived of this one notion: I had no control. This poppy-seed sized being growing within me, fully alive and fully human, yet so extremely fragile and dependent on me—I had absolutely no control over his fate. Besides swallowing down a prenatal vitamin with breakfast, I could do very little to protect the life of this tiny human—my very own child, my flesh and blood. My heart.

> The fear was immense, and it was conceived of this one notion: I had no control.

The night when our first son was born, with lightning flickering in the clouds outside our hospital room, these fears were cemented within my new mama heart. The lights were dim, and I listened to the faint, rhythmic beeping of the machines around me, their notes rising and falling in tandem with my contractions. The nurse stood, staring at that machine. She paged the doctor, and within moments the room was swarming with physicians. Our boy's heart rate dropped dangerously low. The doctor instructed me to change positions, and gently helped me onto my hands and knees. My hospital gown draped around me, doing a very poor job of covering my swollen body. My husband stroked my arm, surely feeling as helpless as I did in that moment. Tears streamed down my face as doctors raced to get our son's heart rate back up, and my heart constricted with this type of fear that was becoming all too familiar as I stood at this threshold of motherhood. I had no control. None of us do.

How do we stand tall when these worries seem so much taller? How do we choose to be brave when the fears come at us without relent? "Do not be afraid of sudden fear," we read in Proverbs 3:25 (NASB). And in these words we are given a boiled-down, condensed glimpse into our real enemy here: fear itself.

Do not be afraid of fear. Traced back to the Hebrew roots of the words, this verse could be written: *Do not be dreadful of sudden terror.* What does this battle look like in the nitty-grittiness of our day-to-day as fear tries its best to constrict and drown us? We must make this choice—*do not be afraid*—every single day, multiple times a day, even. And that choice is made by what we decide to set our eyes and minds to. Our greatest defense as parents battling fear is to submerge ourselves in the goodness of God's Word. By regularly taking in words such as "Do not be afraid of sudden fear," as well as these:

> But he who listens to me shall live securely, and will be at ease from the dread of evil. (Proverbs 1:33 NASB)

> Peace I leave with you; my peace I give you. I do not give to you as the world gives. Do not let your hearts be troubled and do not be afraid. (John 14:27)

> Have I not commanded you? Be strong and courageous. Do not be afraid; do not be discouraged, for the Lord your God will be with you wherever you go. (Joshua 1:9)

> The Lord is my shepherd, I shall not want. He makes me lie down in green pastures; He leads me beside quiet waters. He restores my soul; He guides me in paths of righteousness for His name's sake. Even though I walk through the valley of the shadow of death, I fear no evil, for You are with me; Your rod and Your staff, they comfort me. (Psalm 23:1–4 NASB)

These verses are a drop in the bucket when it comes to the bounty of Scriptures instructing us not to fear, and these along with many others hold the power to extinguish the fears that are trying to hijack our parenthood.

• ◦ • ◦

When we are children ourselves, we believe that our parents hold so much control, that they have everything figured out and managed. But then we become parents and realize how wrong we were. We think that when we are handed that tiny bundle, we'll be handed this new power to keep that itty-bitty human alive and well, and everything we will need to give that child success. We are wrong.

On that night that I became a mother, after a frightening labor with a team of doctors racing to bring our boy's heart rate back up, and then twenty minutes of swift pushing, the doctor placed my son into my arms. I had assumed that this moment when I first set eyes on my child would be filled with relief. I had not lost him. He had made it those months in my womb when I couldn't see him, touch him, or know for certain that he was safe and perfectly well. We had made it.

Yet as I brought him for the first time to my breast and studied every little bit of him, that relief never came. Instead, now that he was here, tiny and fragile and fresh and with 936 weeks before us to spend together, I realized that this was just the beginning. Having him inside me was the safest I would ever feel during our time of raising him. Now, with him outside of the comfort and protection of my womb, he looked terribly vulnerable, exposed to this world and all of its dangers. And in the years to come as he would learn to roll, then crawl, then walk, then run, then climb, as he would ride his bicycle back and forth in the yard and come in at night with skinned knees and bruises, I would see it—that so much of parenthood is made up of faith. And that the battle against fear requires that we daily take up our shield of defense that is God's promises. If we are to find victory over the fear of what we cannot control, then we will need to place these truths before our eyes, and we must do it often. As we do, we'll find that fear, when it shows its ugly face, holds less power over us. The act of setting God's promises in front of our eyes sets them in stone in our hearts.

In the face of what we cannot control, we must believe that God has instructed us over and over again in His Word *Do not fear* for a reason. We must believe in a God who loves our babies so much more than we can grasp, in a God of unwavering faithfulness, in a God who has everything under control.

I sought the Lord, and He answered me; he delivered me from all my fears. (Psalm 34:4)

The Shattered Jar

I pushed the pen into the paint on the wall, made a small indent and a black swirl. I placed the point of a tiny nail into the mark and pounded it in gently. Zeke lay perched up on his elbows on the top level of the bunk bed his daddy had made with his own hands. I placed the level firmly against the nail, swiveling it slightly back and forth until the bubble settled into the middle of the yellow liquid-filled tube. I penned another mark on the wall. "Thank you for celebrating our room, Mom!" my boy exclaimed. I smiled at his use of *celebrate* instead of *decorate*. But even his charming comment could not alleviate the heaviness in my heart. I hung a painting on the nails: a black bear against white wood, and the words, "Be brave, little one." My son smiled. My spirit suffocated.

Since my first days as a mom, I have intentionally chosen to avoid the news. Part of me feels guilty for this. *Shouldn't I be aware of what is going on in the world around me?* Another part of me recognizes this as a survival tactic. There have been times that I have become engrossed in news stories, or even just clicked to open an interesting headline, and found myself devastated. Because what do moms do when they read an article about a child? They insert their own child into the story. They ask, "What if it had been us?" They imagine the pain. The shock. The grief.

And that is just what I had done.

The week had been penetrated with unthinkable stories in the news. Evil prevailing, lives taken, families shattered. And not only evil, but also chance. Another story left my spirit crumpled on the floor, my heart completely sick for a mother who lost her boy in a matter of unimaginable moments.

I picked up another painting and eyed which wall to hang it on. Zeke watched carefully. And I imagined mamas I did not know walking into empty bedrooms, taking in the toys still strewn about and beds still unmade. I imagined their despair at the realization of a bed never to be filled again with the weight of their little one. My heart ached for them, and my spirit constricted at the fearful realization of just how fragile life is. We have so much to lose; how do we live with this terrifying reality every single day, while reading stories of how quickly it can all be taken away? When all we have for certain is today, how will that influence how we spend our time? How would we spend today differently if we knew that tomorrow we would not have the chance?

We have today to linger longer in that embrace. To kiss that pudgy little cheek one more time before bed. To sit with her and string beads on a string. To help him construct that new Lego set. To help her with the math problem she's been struggling with, or to take her mind off of it with a trip to the ice-cream shop. We have today to speak truth over them. To tell them how brave and beautiful and wonderful they are. We have today to set down the to-do list, turn off the cell phone, and take a walk together.

After I published our story of the 936 pennies jar on my blog, there was a small grouping of comments and emails that I received and held dear. They were from parents who had suffered tragic loss. Moms and dads who would never have the chance to spend those 936 pennies. Parents whose penny jars had shattered across the floor, leaving their hearts and lives in fragments. These letters were from parents who had buried children in the ground. I read their messages and wept for them. As tears slid down my face and I whispered prayers for their families, the realization began to wash over me that this was an indispensable part of the 936 Pennies message. We are never guaranteed a full jar. We are never promised those 936 weeks.

David penned it in the Psalms: "Lord, make me to know my end, and what is the extent of my days; let me know how transient

I am" (Psalm 39:4 NASB). We are not told the number of our days, for good reason, I am sure. But we are allowed the knowledge of just how fleeting these days are. It is the same reason that many parents tell me that they cannot set up penny jars in their homes: counting time hurts. The knowledge that, as David later penned in Psalm 144:4, "Man is like a mere breath; His days are like a passing shadow" (NASB). It hurts to open our eyes and view our life in this matter. It hurts even more to view our child's life through this lens. And yet, when we do, when we choose to count time, we realize just how precious every single penny inside that jar is.

> When we choose to count time, we realize just how precious every single penny inside that jar is.

I have stood at the memorial services and gravestones of babies who would never open their eyes outside of their mama's wombs. I have watched the faces of those mothers, eyes red and distant, abdomens still swollen. Empty. Longing for more time, for more kicks, for more slight movements just to know that their child was okay.

I have sat next to a dear friend as she shared a story with me. She told me how she had sat at the memorial service for a friend's child, a mother who would never feel the grip of her tiny one's finger around her own. As my friend sat in that service, she rubbed her hand against her own swollen belly, pleading with God to protect the life within her. My friend shared this story with me hours after the memorial service for her own son. The first time he opened his eyes, he saw Jesus. We sat on her couch, watching her toddler son and my own two boys push trucks around in the dirt outside. And as she shared her story with me, I prayed silent prayers over my own unborn child. I was thirty-three weeks pregnant, sitting next to my dear, sweet friend who had just laid her son to rest. It was a sobering reminder of how closely death and life coexist in this world.

In three weeks I would walk into a darkened ultrasound room for a regular checkup, and be sent straight to labor and delivery.

My son's life would be spared by the grace of God and the gift of modern medicine. We would almost lose him. And then I would hold him, watch his tiny chest rise and fall, and feel his warm body resting next to my bare skin. I would thank God for his life, and pray peace over my friend as she walked through the darkest days of her life.

I knew that this heartbreaking side of the message had to be shared. But how would I, someone who could not begin to fathom that sort of pain, ink sufficient words to walk alongside the grieving? How could I, unfamiliar with the crushing pain of loss, share words that would encourage every parent to take hold of today, because it is all we have for certain? I was at a loss.

That is, until I became acquainted with that very pain myself.

Their Stories Matter

They smiled at us as they walked by, watching the escapade playing out in our dual shopping carts. Mine was piled high with food; my husband's was piled high with our three boys. "This will be you soon!" the gentleman motioned to his cart, stacked over the edges with bulk-sized boxes of food. He and his wife smiled again at our boys, then he joked, "You'll get there eventually. We have four boys and one girl." He meant it in kindness. After all, there was no way he could have known that only hours before I had miscarried our fourth child. I held myself together until my husband and I finished loading our groceries into the back of our SUV. Then he turned to embrace me, and a fresh set of tears began making their way down my face.

Some of us never get the chance to hold that jar of 936 pennies. Some of us hold it only for a moment. Some of us only get the chance to invest a few precious pennies. We knew about our baby for two short days. We were surprised, to say the least. The faint second line on the pregnancy test came shortly after our decision to be done at three boys. My husband and I spent two days rearranging future plans, reorganizing priorities, and making space in our minds for another child. We were shaken, but we were also excited. Nothing could prepare me for the shock that would follow two days later when the blood appeared.

And nothing could ready me for the sea of emotions that would overtake me in the days that followed. I would lay in bed avoiding life, resurfacing above my grief just long enough to pour the baby a bottle or set out Play-Doh for the bigger boys. I did what all women in this shattered state of heart do—I searched for an answer. What could have happened? *Did* this really happen? Again and again I came across this explanation: that an early miscarriage is common. Research stated across the internet, I suppose in a failed attempt to comfort wrecked mothers like myself, that some 70 percent of miscarriages happen in the first weeks of pregnancy. It's normal, everyone said.

But there is nothing normal about losing a child.

Nothing could ready me for the sea of emotions that would overtake me.

There is nothing normal about a lifetime of hopes unraveling in a single moment of despair. There is nothing ordinary about 936 weeks never realized.

One of the emails I received shortly after I shared the 936 Pennies story on my blog was from a mother walking through the grief of losing her daughter. Nicole shared with me:

> I prayed for my daughter long before she was actually conceived. I prayed and planned out just how I would use those pennies. I also started to journal the day after I found out she was in my womb, and continued to prepare and longed for the days I would spend my pennies. . . . I promised God I would spend them wisely.
>
> The morning I went into labor I anxiously awaited meeting that sweet baby—that day would mark the first 1/7 of a penny I'd spend, and I was never more ready. What a day that turned out to be!
>
> A mere 15 hours later I would realize that I wasn't going to get 936 pennies. . . . I didn't even know if I'd get one.
>
> I didn't.
>
> I got just under 2/7 of a penny—at least that's the time she was here on earth. Unexpectedly I had 36 hours to spend all the pennies I could. We talked, had a couple heart-to-hearts,

she was cuddled and read stories, she was prayed over and baptized, and she was told she was loved as we prayed "Now I lay me down to sleep" before she was carried off to Jesus by His angels. . . .

That was late this summer, and I pray often that someday I'm blessed enough to receive another child from God, another jar of pennies and another chance to spend and invest wisely. I don't know how many pennies we'll get through, but I pray I can make them count.

I have followed this mother's journey and prayed for her ever since receiving her message. I have thought of her often, and that single fraction of a penny she was given—her resolve, in the midst of great, unexpected heartache—to spend it the best she could. Since the time that she sent me this email, God has blessed Nicole with another child and another jar of pennies. And just as she wrote to me in that email, she doesn't know how many pennies she'll get through. None of us know for certain the time that we will have with our child. But just as she ended her email, we must pray that we will make those pennies count.

This woman was not the only one to share with me a story of tragic loss. There were many others. Comments on my blog and emails in my inbox left me teary-eyed as I read stories of penny jars that would never be spent. Stories like these are more prevalent than we realize, but there is nothing common about them. Each story is drenched in grief. Each story is about a mother and father, a family, a child. And each of these stories matter.

For the mothers to whom this story belongs, it wasn't only a few days or months of hope and anticipation that they lost. It was a childhood. It was years of tucking in, bedtime prayers, and good-night kisses. If she has other children, she lost a sibling, a best friend, and a confidant for her kids. She didn't lose a wish or a dream. She lost a child.

All of us know someone who has lost a child. In fact, I am certain that we are unaware of much of the grief buried deep within those around us. It is a silent grief. If you have been spared this kind of loss, you might find yourself a bit at a loss as you walk alongside a grieving friend. Speaking from my own loss, one of the greatest ways that you can comfort a grieving parent is by acknowledging their lost child.

Remember that your friend's loss is something that she will feel for the rest of her days. The absence of her child and the loss of opportunity to spend those 936 pennies will weigh heavy on her heart for the remainder of her days. Send a care package, a text message, or a letter just to let her know that you are thinking about her and praying for her. And then, a few months down the road, when the world has moved on but she remains in the depth of silent grief, send another care package, another text message, another note or letter, to assure her that she is not alone and her child will never be forgotten.

In the weeks following the loss of our baby, I began to realize how buried this grief is in our society. We talk about it so little—the early loss of a baby. How insignificant the loss can be made out to be. All of us who have experienced this devastation need to know that it is okay to feel alone and angry and raw and numb and shaken. All at the same time. And that it is not okay to feel embarrassed or ridiculous for those feelings. We need to know that we are not overreacting. We need to be given permission to grieve. And that permission may need to come from ourselves.

We need to know that it will be okay, but that it doesn't have to be okay right now. Instead, right now it is okay for us to bury our face in a pillow and cry. Hard. We need to know that it is okay to curse the cramps in our abdomen and the bloat in our stomach, lingering reminders of what almost was. We need to know that it is okay to scratch everything off our calendar and take a walk. A nap. A shower. A break.

Dear friend, if this story is yours, you need to know this: You are not alone. Whether you held your child in your womb for a few hours, a few days, or some weeks, those intense emotions threatening to overtake you around every corner—you are allowed to feel those. This life that happened and then ended before you hardly knew what was taking place—it mattered. However long you held him or her in your womb or in your arms—your baby mattered.

Each of those jars of pennies is a legacy, no matter how many or few we get to invest.

Resting Secure

The sky was clear and a brilliant blue. The sun cast warmth down from its pedestal, unaware of the impending trauma that would mark my motherhood forever with regret and fear. The scene about to unfold was one that I would regularly have to practice pushing out of my mind in the years to come. There are memories etched into our parenthood that forever tarnish our view of ourselves as mothers and fathers. They are defining instances. They leave their trace of scar and stain upon our souls, arising in our minds at the most unsuspecting moments, waiting to shatter our hearts into pieces over mistakes made. These are the almost tragedies, our greatest fears realized right before our eyes.

Our second-born was four months old. He looked up at me from his car seat as I hoisted it into the back of our Jeep. I assumed my husband was watching our two-and-a-half-year-old. We were new at parenting more than one child and hadn't yet mastered the communication practice of knowing who was watching which child. That is where we made our almost-tragic mistake. As I snapped Ellis's car seat into place, I turned to Ezekiel. My eyes scanned the small expanse of our front yard and failed to find his unruly head of white-blond curls, and my heart stopped. The whole world stopped, really. Most parents have experienced this, a moment when a child cannot be found and all of your greatest fears freeze you dead in your tracks. If you haven't yet experienced this, then I am assuming your child is not yet mobile. You'll get there, and when it happens, your world will cease from spinning—especially if there is a road nearby. In this case, there was.

I leapt to the back of the car to confirm my all-consuming horror. There, my son of not-yet three years old, stood unaware of the danger or the fact that my heart had stopped beating within my chest. Those curls danced softly atop his head as he stood waving to me from across the busy street. My breath held in my lungs and my eyes darted from left to right. Silently I pleaded for no cars to come and that he would stay put rather than run to me. And then I ran. I ran across that road and swept him into my arms, knowing full well that I could have lost him. With one overlook, with one neglect of communication, with one distraction, we could have lost our son in a span of moments. In the years that followed, each time I would think of those minutes, my eyes would cloud with tears and my breath catch in my lungs.

Never before that moment had I realized just how delicate life is, how quickly we can lose everything. When we first bring them home from the hospital, we wonder just how we are supposed to keep that tiny, frail being alive for eighteen years. And with those moments—those close calls that we can never erase from our memory—we are once again confronted with this reality of how much is completely out of our control, and of how quickly that jar of 936 pennies can fall, shattering on the ground. Never to be invested. Forever lost.

One of our biggest challenges as moms and dads is to wage war against the fears that threaten to hijack our parenthood. Motherhood has provided me with a crash course on fear. I thought that perhaps as time went on and I became more comfortable in my new role as a mom, the fears would lose their power. I was very wrong. Each time we brought home a baby from the hospital, my fear grew exponentially in power. The anxieties developed in strength and magnitude. As Lisa-Jo Baker puts it in her book *Surprised by Motherhood*, "With each new baby, we are that much more vulnerable to having our hearts broken into tiny little bits forever. . . . Against all odds, knowing that sickness, sin, failure, and disaster lurk on the fringes of every day, we choose to embrace life."[1]

This was the trick. Rather, this was the high calling—to embrace life to its fullest despite the fears. We as parents are tasked with the job of stripping the worry and panic of its hold on us. And we can only do this by laying those fears—time and time and time again—at the feet of Jesus.

Battling fear is a practice. We try and try again, we fail and succeed, we gain traction one day only to feel engulfed the next—but we keep showing up. We keep practicing. We keep laying our fears, every time they show up, at the feet of Jesus.

After I lost sight of my son on that day, I had a choice. I could allow my mind to wander into the treacherous fields of what-could-have-been, or I could leave it behind us on that curb.

> Each time we brought home a baby from the hospital, my fear grew exponentially in power.

I could suffocate under the terrifying images of what could have happened, relenting to their powerful hold over my spirit—or I could choose to trust Jesus. After all, had He not just proven himself as my son's protector? Had He not just shown me that in those moments when we look away from our child for a moment, His eyes are still locked on them?

That has been one of the most powerful weapons for me in this battle against fear. When my mind begins to wander into those what-if and what-could-have-been territories, I turn my thoughts instead to the countless times and the magnitude of ways in which God has protected my children. I set my heart on this pattern that He has given, on the history of faithfulness He has inscribed into our story so far.

It has not been easy, and in years to come, with more mistakes being added to my motherhood résumé, it would continue to prove a challenge, but I knew that I needed to choose trust over fear. It was the only way. And on one ordinary morning I stumbled upon a gem of truth that would forever alter my view on fear.

There are bits and pieces of God's Word that I wonder deep within my soul if I will ever quite understand. Despite my childhood years spent in church, youth groups, and home Bible studies, despite a couple years of Bible college, despite my own studies of God's Word scattered across early mornings stretching from junior high and into adulthood, there are promises I can't comprehend. I don't know how they work. Yet oddly enough, in their abstract mystery, I find comfort in them. They are promises such as the words of Solomon, the wisest man on earth, personifying wisdom, as if she—wisdom—were speaking directly to our souls, and this is what she offers us: "But whoever listens to me will live in safety and be at ease, without fear of harm" (Proverbs 1:33). In seventeen words, God, speaking in wisdom through Solomon, breathes this promise with traces of solitude, making their way through the tangles of our hearts and unlacing fear's hold on us. In this promise we find our own breath again. We find room to exhale and regroup. We find space to trust.

But how do we *listen to wisdom*? I witnessed this in a very simple way when our middle son was three years old. We were just returning to a trailhead after a two-mile hike with our boys. The sun was descending, and the air grew chillier by the moment. Tummies were grumbling for dinner and feet were weary. But the evening was breathtaking. And as we descended the last hill of our hike, we could hear coyotes calling down below in the prairie lands. It was an eerie and beautiful melody of nature. I glanced back at Ellison, and concern was painted across his face. He had harbored a fear of coyotes since last summer, when he would often hear them calling out in the fields behind our home. As we rounded the last bend in the trail, we assured him that the coyotes were far away.

Minutes later, with the boys strapped into their seats, I spotted one of the coyotes skipping across the prairie grass as we drove down the road. My husband pulled off to the side and we unbuckled Ellison and brought him into the front seat with us for a better view. "See, buddy?" I assured him. "They are just like dogs. They're wild, so we stay away from them, but they are no bigger than our dog."

"Oh!" Ellis exclaimed with a smile on his face as he watched the coyote prowl across the field in search of some dinner. Watching our boy watch the coyote, that is when I realized that until that moment, he did not know what a coyote was. He had only heard their eerie calls echoing into the night but never had a shape or size to attach those noises to. Now, with better understanding, his fears dissipated.

I have found this same truth in my parenthood. Fears feed off of what we do not understand. And as we come time and time and time again to God's Word—*as we listen to wisdom*— **Fears feed off of what we do not understand.** we gain a better understanding of God's power over fears. We understand more just how sovereign and powerful and loving He is. When we place His Word in front of us, He grants us a spirit of wisdom. God's Holy Spirit goes to work in disclosing His truths to us.

Just as Jesus assured His disciples before He went to the cross, He tells us in His Word,

> But the Helper, The Holy Spirit, whom the Father will send in my name, He will teach you all things and bring to your remembrance all that I said to you. Peace I leave with you; My peace I give to you; not as the world gives, do I give to you. Let not your hearts be troubled, neither let them be afraid.
>
> John 14:26–27 esv

When we come regularly to God's Word, with our own spirits attuned to His wisdom, the Spirit teaches us through the truths within it, and we experience more and more that deep, inexplicable peace of Christ. Fear has no place, and we learn to rest secure, free from the dread of disaster.

Unwavering Faithfulness

One morning when our oldest boys were two and three, as I sat in our study stringing words together on a screen, I welcomed the distraction of giggles resonating from their bedroom across the house. It was early, and they were waking one another up with their playful chatter. I love this about them—that at such a young age, when they could hardly communicate with us, they had their own little world and vocabulary with each other. Each morning I get to relish in their cheerful voices as they begin to embrace the day and its adventures.

I sat for a moment trying to make out their stories, and as I did I opened an email. It was a church member asking for prayer for friends, a couple ushering their twenty-year-old son into hospice care as he faced his last days of cancer. Twenty years old, all of their 936 pennies spent, but still a life cut short. I closed my eyes and listened to my own boys with still so many pennies remaining in their jars, and I tried not to imagine it.

But that is what mothers do; we hear a story of tragedy and loss, and we place ourselves in the situation, try to imagine the pain, the loss, the impossibility of it all. We are crazy for doing this, but it is what we do. It's the same craziness that causes a slight panic in me whenever my husband and the three boys go out together, offering me some quiet time of rest. Yes, the solitude is wonderful, but part of me can't help but think: What if they get into an accident and I lose all four of them? It's ludicrous, of course—or is it? We read the stories and we know these things happen. What is to keep them from happening to us?

When we hear accounts of others' real and raw tragedy, we try to wish it all away. We say a quick prayer for the stranger—the one actually wading through the depths of this tragedy—and we will ourselves to move on, thankful that it is not us. All around I see it. All of us do, as friends lose babies, children, and adult children. We live in a fallen and tragic world where no one upon learning of the child growing in their womb is guaranteed a jar 936 pennies full. Some will never have the chance to spend that first penny. Some, like my husband and I, will only know about their child for mere days before realizing that those pennies will never be spent. Others will hold their child and gaze into their eyes for a few days, a few weeks, a few months, or a few years. There is no guarantee of how many pennies we will get to spend with our children. Nine hundred and thirty-six is the best-case scenario, but what do we do with that knowledge?

I'm left with the inevitable question: What does this mean for my own parenting journey while I still have these pennies to spend? While I still have this week? While I still have this day? They say you should spend each day as if it is your last. Part of this I see as wise—that we spend each day with our child with the full knowledge that we are not guaranteed another with them. But we also must not give up hope. We must spend each penny as if we will have that time, because we need to invest in it. We need to use the day we have today in order to create something beautiful for the remainder of the days we are afforded.

What does this mean? What does it look like in the midst of real parenting? It means enjoying the moment, taking every moment as a gift and turning around to invest it to its fullest potential. It means that when we are with our child, we need to be fully there, taking in their details, searching their hearts, and understanding and enjoying them for who they are. It also means that we realize that although we don't know how many pennies we will have, we press on in hope and live as good stewards of the time we have, even though we are uncertain of its length. We spend the penny we have this week so that the penny we spend next week will be even more full of life and love. Each penny sets the next penny up for more potential.

And we don't live in fear.

When we hear the stories, when we see the grieving, we grieve along. We pray, and then we give thanks for the mercy we've been shown as we hold that tiny child with heart still beating and flesh still flush with life. We thank God for that, because it is a gift, one we have so much responsibility to invest in. We learn from those who have endured great loss—those who had only one fraction of a penny, and who know just how valuable each copper coin truly is. And we move forward with all resolve to not squander one single cent, because some are not even given that chance.

> How might I spend each penny so that none are taken for granted, but each one is seen as a gracious gift from God?

It is in these stories—and in my own after the loss of our baby—that I am challenged in my everyday mothering to reflect on time I have already spent. I look at last week—a whole penny spent—and I must ask myself if my investment was wise. Was it beautiful? Did it bestow life? Did it pass on to my child lessons in how to live abundantly? How might I spend each penny so that none are taken for granted, but each one is seen as a gracious gift from God?

In her book *Anchored*, author Kayla Aimee shares with startling honesty her story of when she gave birth to her daughter three and a half months early. Her daughter weighed only one pound and eight ounces, and Kayla could not even hold her until she was a month old. At one point she stood watching in horror as her daughter hung between life and death, a flat line on a black monitor speaking her worst nightmares. She left her readers with this conclusion on the fragility of life: "Everything I have is utterly intangible, a knowing that was still and small and aching.

As I stood there at the glass, I knew that if I walked back into that room only to find myself holding her lifeless form against my still beating heart, everything else would change and God would not."[2]

Every day she watched as her daughter, with fingers no wider than a grain of rice, fought to live one more moment, one more hour. Her realization that God is unchanging came in a moment of trauma, but it was born of an immense struggle Kayla faced as she attempted to make sense of faith and love and prayer in the midst of an unbelievable trial.

I like to believe that if this young woman with wavering faith could trust in God's unchanging character in the face of such pain, that maybe I could also if I were to endure such a tragedy. Her anchor, the truth that God will never change, can be traced straight back to Scripture: "If we are faithless, He remains faithful, for he cannot disown himself" (2 Timothy 2:13).

We can't understand why some tragedies take place. But we can know that God will never become less faithful. He can't, because to do so would be to go against His very nature. When we anchor ourselves in what we know to be true of God—that He is good and loving and powerful, and that He desires good for us—we find space to breathe again. If I am ever to behold my son on an operating table, or see him the victim of senseless violence, or feel my heart tear in two as he fights for life, I know this one sure thing: God is unchanging. His faithfulness, even when I cannot see it, remains steadfast and true.

I don't understand why babies die. I can't comprehend why some new mothers are wheeled out of the hospital with "Congratulations!" balloons floating above the wheelchair armrest and a bundle of life cradled in their arms, while other mothers leave with only a couple of photos and a heart forever shattered and aching. It is far beyond me to fathom these things. But this one thing I do know: God's faithfulness is unwavering. That has to be enough. Enough for the mother weeping before a tiny gravestone, and enough for all of us as we battle that same haunting fear every single day. He is enough, and as we begin to trust in that one unchanging truth, we will discover great peace and confidence to live unafraid.

> Light dawns in the darkness for the upright;
>   he is gracious, merciful, and righteous . . .
> For the righteous will never be moved . . .
> He is not afraid of bad news;
>   his heart is firm, trusting in the LORD.
> His heart is steady; he will not be afraid.
>
> Psalm 112:4–8 ESV

Questions to Reflect On

- What types of fears are threatening to hijack your parenthood today? What news sites, social media feeds, blogs, television shows, or other sources are fueling these fears? Replace them today with God's Word.

- Are you consumed by what-if or what-could-have-been fears? Make a list of specific ways that God has proven himself as the Protector of your family.

-seven-
Navigating
Time

Desperate for Answers

His scream pierced the air, his voice stricken with fear. Even from a floor away in the house, it perforated space and went straight into my innermost being. My mama heart knew that cry; he was scared—and I ran.

Bounding down those stairs, my mind raced with the dreadful possibilities—the scenarios that play out in all of our minds when we know our child is afraid. I found him huddled in a corner, shaking. The child sitter who was watching the children during our Bible study stood next to him, trying to calm him, unaware of what had triggered his reaction. I scooped him up and held him near. I tried to soothe his frantic heart, but without understanding the source of his fear, my comfort for him was painfully limited.

It had begun months earlier at Thanksgiving. The adults had all been gathered in the kitchen, laughing the evening away in sweet fellowship. My parents had rented a large cabin on a ranch where all of us could spend the week. Our son slept soundly in a side bedroom. He had been asleep for hours; we hadn't heard a peep from his room, but then with a bout of laughter from the kitchen, he jostled awake and began to scream. I had rushed into the room to find him sitting up in his Pack 'n Play, terrified and shaking. I lifted him up and pulled him tight against me, willing the warmth of my embrace to calm his terrors. In my own frenzied state, I tried to assess his fear. My first thought was that he was having a seizure, with the way his body convulsed. My eyes darted from him to the other room. "Grayson!" My own voice shook with panic as I cried for my husband to come quickly. My boy continued to shake in my arms, awake but unresponsive to me. My husband came quickly, and along with him a dear family friend who was spending the week with us. She drew near and placed her hand on my son, and began praying God's power over him. She prayed for peace, and I begged it for my own soul, as well.

Now, months later in our friend's home, as I held him up against me, smoothing back his hair and swaying gently, my own heart raced. This was just one more thing—one more unknown—one more unexplainable outburst of fear we had seen from him over the past several months. I didn't know how much more my heart could take as fear tightened its vile grip around me.

Over recent months we had begun to notice that loud noises sent our son into a frenzy. I would cautiously glance at him before turning on the blender. Immediately tears would spring to his eyes as he would call out in fear, and I would turn it off and run quickly to console him. The vacuum generated hysteria. I knew this all to be somewhat normal behavior for a two-year-old, yet something in my gut told me this was more than that. It wasn't only noise. At times he would come running from his room, screaming with no explanation. The fear only compounded as he fell further and further behind in his speech development. Trying to understand a simple sentence from him was exhausting; trying to understand the demons behind his fears was nearly impossible.

My mind was consumed by the haunting possibilities: Had someone hurt him? Was he suffering from night terrors? Did his sensitivity to sensory stimulation stem from a mental illness?

As I held my shaking boy, my spirit ached for answers. When would these fears relent? When would I understand his anxiety? And the question that weighed the heaviest on me: When would I finally understand how to help him? In the confusion and angst of the unknown, I felt helpless to soothe my child's tortured soul.

Fear has that way about it. Upon its arrival, it always brings with it a suitcase full of questions. And then it slowly and strategically inserts those questions into our minds. *Am I doing something wrong? Did something bad happen that I don't know about? Am*

I offering him enough security? Does he feel loved unconditionally? Is he suffering from some emotional trauma? We ask them all. And as we do, we begin to lose grip on our own security. We doubt our love, our affection, our parenting strategies, and our own qualifications for this calling.

That evening at the Bible study, we were newcomers. It had been only a few months since we had moved to Missouri, and only a few weeks since we had stumbled into this small family of believers that we were quickly finding ourselves fond of. I had befriended our pastor's wife; her own son was the same age as our firstborn, the two boys born on the very same day states apart, bound to become buddies. I still didn't know her well, but I knew that she had taught in a school for children with developmental setbacks.

Questions teetered on the tip of my tongue, begging to be asked, begging for some clarity, but fear had held me back from asking them. I was terrified of what the answers might bring. This time, however—with my boy trembling and inconsolable in my arms—pushed those questions over the edge. I needed wisdom, and knew that this new friend likely had some in this area. Later that night, when my son had calmed, I broached the subject nonchalantly with her. I tried to mask the fear in my words. I fought hard to keep my voice from breaking.

"He's been sensitive lately . . . to noise. He's had these irrational fears." I asked about early signs of autism—I asked coldly, as if I were writing a report on the subject, not as if I feared these sufferings in my own son. I didn't understand this fear, or how it gripped me so ruthlessly. Around every corner it taunted me, whispering "What if . . . ?" at every unusual behavior my child exhibited. I didn't know what to do, and my lack of understanding and direction left me wrought with anxiety; I was paralyzed in fear—not much unlike my own son. It can be nearly impossible to remain calm and step forward when we have no idea what direction to take, or even how we got to where we find ourselves.

I was sure that my friend sensed my fear—she is a mother, too, after all. She responded with sound knowledge from her own education and experience, and explained to me the facts—exactly what I needed, and what to watch for. Her words provided the start to a foundation, something firm and sound to pull myself up onto. But still my emotions shook that ground as I tried to steady my feet upon something sure.

I broke down in tears on the way home. My husband pulled the car over. Our boys chattered together playfully from the backseat. He rubbed my back, assured me our son was fine. I wasn't convinced. That evening I typed out an email to my sister. She had worked as a teacher's aid in a school for autistic children. Again I tried to mask my fear—again I am sure that it screamed loudly from behind my typed words. She is a mother, as well, and she sensed what I needed: hard facts. I needed to know how I could be certain if something was wrong. She told me what to look for and tried to calm my nerves. Knowledge has a way of equipping us, emboldening us, and enabling us to walk forward with some sense of direction. But there is something else about knowledge—it can only go so far. Knowledge is made of facts and truth. But we need wisdom in order to interpret that knowledge into everyday life application. I now had the facts, but I needed God's Spirit to show me what to do with them.

My feet were sunk down deep in the mire of terror, and I was far too weak to lift them out onto solid ground. If I was to rise out of this pit of fear, I would need more than only knowledge—I was in urgent need of wisdom. And so I did the only thing I knew to do: I prayed for wisdom. I didn't even know what, exactly, I was praying for, but I stood upon a promise I knew to be sure: that God grants wisdom to those who ask for it in faith. As James puts it, "If any of you lacks wisdom, let him ask God, who gives generously to all without reproach, and it will be given him. But let him ask in faith, with no doubting" (1:5–6 ESV).

In those times when we have no idea how to move forward, when we're paralyzed from making the next move, prayer is the answer. Sometimes there is a lot of waiting involved. Always there is much faith required. In the waiting time is when fears haunt—yet wisdom has a way of snuffing out those fears. The author of Proverbs personifies wisdom, giving wisdom a voice to speak into our souls. She says, "I love those who love me, and those who seek me diligently find me" (8:17 ESV). This is when wisdom digs deep, uprooting all of who we've been and creating us new. It cultivates and grows around us a hedge of protection. It weaves within our hearts a tenacious fabric of confidence. It maps out within our spirit the way we ought to follow—the course attuned to God's own heart. It erases years of fear, insecurity, and confusion, and replaces them with a firm and overwhelming peace. This wisdom not only guides us, but it also breathes new life straight into the deadest parts of us.

> In those times when we have no idea how to move forward . . . prayer is the answer.

• • • •

We had our son evaluated. I prayed that nothing would come of it, but I also prayed for sure answers. His evaluation came back clear; no signs of mental illness, only a delay in speech, which we had already been aware of.

Something happened in all of this praying and waiting. We began to notice that his behavior was normalizing—well, whatever that means for a two-year-old. He was still sensitive to loud and abrupt noises, but a simple covering of the ears sufficed over screams of terror.

And something else began to happen, as well, something monumental to my motherhood: I began to understand my son. For one, his ability to communicate progressed. With his new words and his growing understanding of emotions, he began to communicate with us. We were able to piece together the fragments of his fears; they stemmed from what he didn't understand. His growing imagination had left empty pockets in his conception of the world around him—and those hollow spaces of his perception had begun filling with fears. Slowly we began to dig deep to reach those pockets, unearth those fears, and uproot them with knowledge, peace, and truth. Over time we worked to calm his heart by first understanding his mind.

When we were still in the thick of his fears and the thick of our own, the task of navigating the road before us seemed impossible. It was uncharted territory, and I felt as though my son's soul rested on our decisions—the ones I had no idea how to make. As we worked hard to replace his fears with understanding, I began to look back, and that is when I saw it: traces of God's faithfulness. Around every bend, He was equipping us with wisdom. The same path, looking forward from the beginning, was dark and filled with uncertainty and fear. Now, glancing back at where we had come from, I saw God's clear guidance throughout our steps. He had been faithful to answer our prayers—our desperate pleas—for wisdom. As we took steps forward in prayer and the pursuit of wisdom, He had cleared the way for us. Through this process He was not only rescuing my son from fear and transforming me as a mother, He was also teaching me something of great magnitude that I would fiercely need for the rest of our time raising these boys—an understanding for navigating the path before us, and a promise of guidance. He was assuring me that He was already ten steps ahead of us. He could see our penny jar completely spent, and He was showing us daily how to best spend them. He does the same for each of us on this parenthood journey, if we'll come to His Word, bend our knees in prayer, and ask for wisdom. He is faithful to grant it.

> For the Lord gives wisdom; from his mouth come knowledge and understanding. He holds success in store for the upright, he is a shield to those whose walk is blameless, for he guards the course of the just and protects the way of his faithful ones. Then you will understand what is right and just and fair—every good path. For wisdom will enter your heart, and knowledge will be pleasant to your soul.
>
> Proverbs 2:6–10

"Was This the Right Move?"

I sat across from my husband at a cafe in downtown Milwaukee, Wisconsin. Our only boy was home being watched by friends, and my belly was swollen with our second son, due in mere weeks. I picked up a grape and dipped it in cream cheese spread. Grayson sipped his coffee. The morning was unrushed and a break from our normal routine. We had always wanted to try this restaurant. But it wasn't only the eggs Benedict and house-made veggie sausage that brought us there that morning. We had an agenda. I pulled out my journal and a pen.

Within a couple of hours we would draw up a plan of sorts. A date would be chosen, a deadline for making an even grander decision—one laid before the Lord that would lead us, before the year's end, to a new state and a fresh beginning. We knew that God wanted us to take a next step. And we told Him that within one month's time, we would take that step, and that we were trusting Him during that time to guide us in which direction to begin walking. In essence, we said, "Lord, in one month, we'll begin packing our bags and move to Washington . . . unless you do this one thing. Unless we receive a phone call from this organization with an invite to work with them in Kansas City." We had worked with this mission in the past but had not done much together in years. Our prayer was more of a test, I suppose. "Lord, if Washington is not what you have for us right now, then you're going to have to do this very specific thing to make that clear."

This is one way that my husband and I have approached decision-making in our marriage. We "lay out a fleece." The concept comes from Judges 6, when Gideon lays out a fleece to receive a clear answer from God. "Then Gideon said to God, 'If You will deliver Israel through me, as You have spoken, behold, I will put a fleece of wool on the threshing floor. If there is dew on the fleece only, and it is dry on all the ground, then I will know that You will deliver Israel through me, as You have spoken'" (Judges 6:36–39 NASB).

God had already spoken and told Gideon that He would do this great thing, but Gideon wanted more proof before he put himself out there. God is so very patient with our doubts, is He not? He granted Gideon this evidence, and the next morning, when Gideon arose, he "squeezed the fleece, he drained the dew from the fleece, a bowl full of water." But even that was not enough for Gideon. He went again to God, "Do not let you anger burn against me," he said, "that I may speak once more; please let me make a test once more with the fleece." This time Gideon asked for the opposite, that the fleece would be dry and only the ground wet. Again God showed His magnificent patience toward Gideon, and did as Gideon asked. And that morning over coffee and biscuits, we were laying down our own fleece. We were asking for some very clear, specific direction.

A few weeks later, as we drove back roads awaiting my contractions to move closer together, my husband's phone rang, and we had our invitation to Kansas City to work with the mission organization we had named. Just as in Gideon's story, God was so very patient with us, meeting us in our doubts and unbelief, and showing us a clear path to take.

Within six month's time, we were unloading boxes and setting up home in a place we had never envisioned ourselves—but God had. However, our move to Kansas City was anything but smooth, and even after all the prayers, because of our many trials, I would question again and again whether we had made the right move. I am sure that Gideon felt the same way. After God confirmed to him twice through the fleece that he would deliver Israel in battle, Gideon readied the army. And then God condensed his army from 22,000 men to three hundred, and told him to go into battle with only those three hundred men. I'm sure Gideon had his doubts. And I'm guessing his mind was wandering back to that fleece. *Was this really what God had in mind?* That is exactly the question I was asking on the day we moved to Kansas City.

It began when the house we had a contract to purchase fell through two days before our move from Wisconsin. As we trekked across miles upon miles of farmland, we were driving to our new "home," but we were, in essence, homeless. More than once I caught myself wondering if we had heard God correctly. Sometimes we can have such a clear understanding of what we're supposed to do and where we're meant to go, and yet the journey required to arrive there is wrought with doubt-inducing obstacles all along the way.

My husband drove ahead of me in his truck, pulling along a small trailer packed to the brim with everything we owned, which wasn't much. Our firstborn son, two and a half years old at the time, sat next to his daddy, car seat strapped in the passenger seat. For hours he played with the Magna Doodle his grandparents had bought him for the voyage, and watched out the window as the miles passed, unaware that he was leaving behind everything he knew and was heading toward the unknown. I drove behind them in our Jeep Cherokee, our four-month-old son sleeping soundly in the car seat behind me. As I watched the tarp on our trailer ahead of me flap in the wind, I willed myself to think of something other than the friends I was driving away from and the uncertainty that lay ahead.

As we drove, my husband corresponded with an old friend who now lived in Kansas City with her husband. She had learned of our slightly desperate situation, and had taken it upon herself to find us somewhere to stay until we could find another house to purchase.

She told us of an available apartment in her neighborhood that we could move into that day; we wrote down the address. After two long days of travel, we pulled up to our prospective apartment in Kansas City. I call it prospective, but we were painfully aware that it was our only option. As we pulled to the side of the road in front of the old brick three-story building, I observed our surroundings and realized just how downtown we truly were. It was the "sirens welcome you every morning and tuck you in at night" type of downtown.

Over the next five weeks, that apartment would cause me to question our decision every single day. In our desperate situation, it served as a home. And yet with cat-hair-caked carpeting, pigeons in the walls, and a later discovery of bird mites that would plague me with itchy welts day in and day out, we felt anything but "home."

I found solace in warm cups of coffee and French beignets dusted in powdered sugar when we would escape the apartment to venture out and explore our new city. As we drove around in search of new playgrounds, farmers markets, and hiking trails, I would remember that our situation was neither hopeless nor permanent. There was more to our life than where we were living; God had called us to something great—not the misery I'd allowed myself to wallow in.

When circumstances of life dip low and we find ourselves in a place we never anticipated, it seems that one of the first promises we forget is the one that God calls us to great things. He has created each of us with a great purpose, as well as our children. And in order to speak that promise into their lives, we must believe it for ourselves—no matter what life throws at us. We must believe that if God told us to take this step, to make this move, then He has a purpose, and that purpose will prevail against our deepest doubts and discouragements.

Let me be the first to admit that I have struggled with living my life in light of this promise. At times after our move, my anxiety would grow too much to bear. I would succumb to my anguish, allowing it to overtake me. There was just too much disappointment for what was supposed to be a celebratory time in our life. When tears sprung to my eyes, my husband would hold me, console me, assure me we'd be fine; we'd find a home. He was our strength, keeping us afloat in a great sea of uncertainty, and pointing my heart back to the promises of God.

Taking the steps that God lays before us does not always lead us to instant confirmation. Sometimes it leads to greater struggles and deeper questions. Sometimes, after we lay out that fleece, He has some of His own testing in store for us. Will we trust Him when the following gets difficult? When the path grows uncertain, will we settle into His truth and plant our hearts in what we know to be true?

> When the path grows uncertain, will we settle into His truth and plant our hearts in what we know to be true?

God remained true to the promise that He made Gideon, and then assured him again and again through the laying down of the fleece. God delivered Israel in miraculous fashion through Gideon, despite his doubts. God did the same for us through the laying down of our own fleece, that we were to move to Kansas City. He worked in our life above and beyond our questioning.

The funny thing is, through various circumstances, we did not end up working with the mission organization that invited us to Kansas City. God used our fleece, but He had other plans. Despite our questioning whether this was a right move, He worked in incredible ways to confirm within our hearts that He had us right where He wanted us during that time in our life. And in His gracious provision, He gave us a place to call home. As I eagerly packed up our apartment to move into our new house, He reassured my heart that yes, we had made the right move. Despite our doubts and questions, He was guiding us into His best plan for us. Looking back a few years later, we can see vivid reasons why God led us to Kansas City during that time in our life. What was murky and uncertain and frightening at the time looks beautiful from this end.

As we go about spending our 936 pennies, and facing the decisions that they inevitably bring with them, there are so many times that we are tempted to doubt. Our minds and hearts become clouded with questions. *What is God's plan for our family? What if we make a wrong move? Was this the right move?* And yet, as we find in Gideon's story, and as I found in my story, God is patient with our questions and doubts. Just as the father with a demon-possessed son in Mark 9:24 declared, "I do believe; help me overcome my unbelief." God does just that. He is merciful toward our unbelief, and as we learn to heed His spirit and seek wisdom in His word, He helps our unbelief, and He guides us in His plans and paths as we go about our penny spending.

Not-So-Expert Advice

Sometimes we are up against big questions, ones certain to alter the course of our 936 pennies. But sometimes the smaller questions, all adding up, heap themselves upon us as one big overwhelming pile of uncertainty. These are the countless questions that we are asked to answer every single day.

What kind of decisions are you up against right now? Is your season one of, *Do we homeschool, private school, or public school? Should I let her sleep over at that friend's house? Do I take away his car keys for this? Was that bullying, and do I need to call that child's parent?* We are called to make countless decisions throughout our 936 weeks. Some feel insignificant, some monumental, but all thrown together, they can leave us feeling paralyzed. And I have noticed that it is when I feel most suffocated by these questions that I am most vulnerable to seeking answers that might not satisfy. In the midst of endless questions, we also have available to us endless sources of advice and opinions. However, sometimes these sources can be shaky, and when not measured up to God's Word, they can leave us feeling even more stranded than when we first set out to find answers.

● ● ● ●

I recall it vividly, the dark room illuminated only by a small battery-operated touch light glowing next to the empty bassinet. My husband paced our bedroom floor *"shush-shushing"* while bouncing that tiny bundle in his arms. He looked so tired, slumped over, his whole body screaming for rest. I turned over, burying my head in the pillow, willing myself back to sleep, all the while feeling guilty that I was the one afforded the comfort of the mattress right now, even though it would be me pacing the floor in approximately one and a half hours.

Our first son was four months old, and his aptitude for sleeping at night was decreasing rapidly. He had quickly gone from waking two times a night to five. Morning would come far too early, when I would groggily slip his tiny arms into a onesie, strap him into his car seat, and drop him off at the daycare at the Bible college while I went to morning classes. Meanwhile, my husband would put in a full day's work of manual labor at his roofing job, then come home to his own studies for his bachelor's degree. We would then settle into bed with little anticipation of the broken sleep to come. We were at the end of our rope, and our marriage was feeling the strain. We decided we needed a book to fix our woes—and maybe another pot of coffee.

I devoured every word in that book within two days, hungry for a solution to get our child to sleep through the night. We implemented the book's suggestions on getting our son onto a predictable schedule, and within ten days, we were all sleeping through the night!

Just under two years after we transitioned our son to a successful sleep pattern, my belly was swollen with our second son about to arrive. In anticipation—and a bit of fear—I picked up the same book. My plan was to implement its strategies beginning right from the maternity ward, and to have our new boy sleeping blissfully through the night by one month old. I was almost successful in that plan—give or take eight months. It is clear to us now, a few years later, that our second-born is drastically different from our first when it comes to schedule and structure. While our firstborn thrives on predictability, our second drums to the beat of spontaneity. Even with the same strategies in place, he was nine months old before he slept through the night. In a few years' time, our third son would still be interrupting our sleep at nearly two years old.

Basing our strategies on the same advice and suggestions resulted in a wholly different experience from one child to the next.

Advice can be good, but it is just that—advice—a string of opinions and recommendations, with no guarantee to anchor it as a sure thing. Unless we keep this in mind, we set ourselves up for disappointment and frustration. When we lean too heavily on the experience or opinion of someone else, we're bound to fall at some point. And I would rather base my own parenting decisions on sound wisdom and knowledge, guarding myself and our family against those falls throughout our 936 weeks.

I've seen it inundating social media: real mamas in the trenches of sleepless newborn nights, toddler teething, and preschool decisions, these weary women grasping out for other moms to answer their questions with sound experience and advice. And I'm disconcerted when I see

> When we lean too heavily on the experience or opinion of someone else, we're bound to fall at some point.

it. Yes, I see the value in learning from others' experiences, and others who have learned the hard lessons through trial, error, and grace, or else I would never have typed out the first word of this book. It is the dependency that worries me, the assumption that these mothers—myself often included—make in thinking that another mom's experience is enough to lead and guide our own decisions. The truth is this: No expert and no other parent can make the calls for us. Whether we feel like it or not, we are the ones who hold the firsthand experience when it comes to raising our children and understanding their individual needs.

Parents are hungry today more than ever, perhaps because the demands and expectations to raise the next generation into well-rounded, contributing members of society are higher than ever. It's seen in the myriad of books, magazines, blog posts, and other media that tell parents how to do everything "just right," offering promises that can hardly hold up in the face of reality. My fear is that our minds have been compromised in subtle ways and must be refocused on truth—truth that breathes life into our souls and into our families, truth that enables us to give far more than we are ever capable of giving on our own. We need to lean hard into the only foolproof parenting advice, the truth that God gives us in His Word.

Tedd Tripp, in his book *Shepherding a Child's Heart*, says parents are "bowing to the experts who tell them what kind of training their children need."[1] We are eating up this advice from the "experts," all while forgetting that *we* are the expert when it comes to our own child. Somehow we become convinced that if we read the right article and follow the "Five Steps to a More Obedient Child" instructions, then our success as a parent will be secured.

However, you know what makes your own child tick and where their pressure points are. You know your child's weaknesses, insecurities, skills, talents, and pride. Or you'll see these things when you expand time with full attention, and study your child for who they are through engaging in their world. God has gifted us with this front-row knowledge of who our child is, and that insight, paired with the truths and promises found in His Word, are the firmest foundation that we can ever stand upon when making decisions for our families.

I am not against seeking advice on parenthood, not at all. Proverbs 13:20 explains, "Whoever walks with the wise becomes wise" (ESV). I am all for surrounding ourselves with people who have "been there" and successfully raised their children to know, love, and follow the Lord. There is definite value to be found in the experience of a fellow sojourner, and community is critical in our parenting.

Proverbs 15:22 tells us, "Plans fail for lack of counsel, but with many advisers they succeed." Fellow parents often serve as these counselors. My husband and I have always tried to place ourselves around parents who are a few years ahead of us on this journey so that we can reap wisdom from their experience and knowledge. There is so much beauty in the shared experience of parenthood. Doing life alongside other parents has been some of the most beautiful "church" experiences that I have had. As we read in Hebrews 10:24–25, "Let us consider how we may spur one another on toward love and good deeds, not giving up meeting together, as some are in the habit of doing, but encouraging one another." Sometimes these "meeting together" moments look like sharing cups of coffee and conversation with another mom at the park, or having another couple and their children over to dinner. The conversations that happen in these times can be packed full of encouragement and "spurring one another on toward love and good deeds."

I think there is a great danger, however, in expecting too much from others' advice, in anticipating sure results and guaranteed success based on someone else's experience. Rather, I believe the healthy balance is found when we heed the wisdom and experience of others who have gone before us, and then in prayer and deep consideration of our child's uniqueness and our family's current season, apply that wisdom as God's spirit leads us. All the while understanding that there will be trial and error along the way, and we might need to adapt our strategies as we go.

As we travel along this road, I have learned to take every piece of advice with a grain of salt. I am thankful for the shared experience of parenthood and the vast opportunities we have today to share that experience with one another. But we must tread carefully, continuously holding our parenting up and viewing it through the lens of God's truth, rather than the opinions or experience of others.

As we stand complete within Christ's righteousness and seek Him daily for wisdom, then we can be the expert on our child, because it is God giving us the expertise to see into our child's heart and deep down to their real needs.

When it comes to both the big and small questions that fill my mind as a parent—those wonderings that dance in my head every single day as I seek to raise these God-given babies—my prayer is that I will seek the wisdom of God before the wisdom of man. I hope that when I look back on these days, I won't see a fretful me wandering about, floundering from this strategy to that, uncertain of my methods. I hope instead to look back and see, right among the mistakes and mishaps, a sure confidence. I hope to see myself hand-in-hand with my husband, making these decisions unafraid, standing on the firm foundation of God's Word and our front-row observations of our children's hearts, knowing that "the wisdom that comes from heaven is first of all pure; then peace-loving, considerate, submissive, full of mercy and good fruit, impartial and sincere" (James 3:17). This is the wisdom I pray we will draw from all of these days, week after week, until our jar of pennies is spent.

Whatever questions hover in your mind unanswered today, take a moment to step back and take a deep breath. Consider whether you have been placing all of your eggs in the wisdom-of-this-world basket. Have you been banking everything on the opinions and recommendations of social media, books, blogs, and others' experiences—or the sound, peaceable wisdom from God's Word? Although His Word does not offer a quick fix for getting your infant to sleep through the night, or what to do when your daughter comes home and announces she has a date with a boy you're not fond of, God's Word offers much more. It gives us the confidence that we need to raise our children. It meets us right where we are, reminds us that God chose us for a reason to raise this child, and that He will enable us with all that we need for life and godliness. His Word equips us with all that we need to be the expert on our child.

Considering the remainder of the 936 weeks stretched before us with each of our children, there is a whole lot of unknown territory. Those decisions unmade and courses unchosen can look like lofty mountains with impossible passes. But God promises to level the paths before us. We read it in Proverbs 5:21: "For the ways of a man are before the eyes of the Lord, and He watches all his paths" (NASB). Traced back to its roots, the word *watches* does not mean that the Lord sits high up in heaven, distant from our everyday lives, thinking vaguely about the course we are taking as if watching a sitcom unfold. No, *watches* also holds the meaning "to make level" or "smooth."

As we walk this road and learn to balance the advice and opinions of others, including the words you find in this book, we must hold them up to the lens of God's Word. As we do, those daunting mountains begin to look a lot more passable. And always—always—God goes before us.

Promised Land

Their leader was dead. They had every reason to be terrified—especially Joshua, as he was the next in command.

> After the death of Moses the servant of the Lord, the Lord said to Joshua the son of Nun, Moses' aide: "Moses my servant is dead. Now then, you and all these people, get ready to cross the Jordan River into the land I am about to give to them—to the Israelites" (Joshua 1:1–2).

With Moses in the ground, how was Joshua to lead this great people into God's Promised Land—and who was he to do so, anyway?

I sometimes feel this way and find myself asking, *Who am I to lead these children into adulthood? Who am I to nurture them and teach them about love, how to ride a bike, how to respond to a bully, how to make friends, or what to do when those friends hurt you? Who am I to teach them about regret and goodness and justice and living an abundant life?* Yet we are called to navigate them through these years with sound wisdom, and in such a way to usher them into a full and abundant life as an adult.

Maybe you're asking the same question that Joshua did, "Who am I, oh God?" It seems that in the fear of the task, we often forget a beautiful piece to God's calling on our life: His calling is always bound together with a promise. Here was the promise He made to Joshua in those dark and uncertain days: "I will give you every place where you set your foot, as I promised Moses" (v. 3).

God told him to move forward and carry on this great mission—and then promised that He would go before him and pave the way; God would give him the victory! And He promises the same for us. But God didn't stop with the promise—He went on to explain to Joshua just how to follow this calling that God was placing on his life. God gave him the game plan. He instructed him:

> Be strong and very courageous. Be careful to obey all the law my servant Moses gave you; do not turn from it to the right or to the left, that you may be successful wherever you go. Keep this Book of the Law always on your lips; meditate on it day and night, so that you may be careful to do everything written in it. Then you will be prosperous and successful. Have I not commanded you? Be strong and courageous. Do not be afraid; do not be discouraged, for the Lord your God will be with you wherever you go. (vv. 7–9)

The Law—the Word and truth of God—this is what would guide Joshua's every step; this is what would give him the courage he needed to carry out the task. It would also ensure his "good success" in the mission. His Word acts as the same kind of reservoir for us today, upon which we draw peace, wisdom, and direction for this journey.

We stare at those brand-new babes fresh from the womb, wrapped up all warm and soft in fleece blankets, helpless and begging to be nourished, guided, and led to abundant life. It leaves us wondering how, exactly, we are to take every next step correctly so that we end up on the right path of parenthood, guiding our precious children to the life God has for them. It is overwhelming, to say the least—and terrifying.

On that day when I was handed our first penny jar at our son's dedication service, it was like being handed a newborn babe all over again. Only now, with seventy-six pennies already gone, we are already short on time. Those jars. They give me sharp focus and strong conviction, and they challenge me with their relentless message. Time is merciless, and will continue to be spent. And we have a mission as parents to make sure that as that happens, it is being invested in the fullest way possible—in the building of an abundant life for our children.

In a culture that has succumbed to passive parenting, it takes great strength and courage to do things differently at the expense of looking authoritarian, strict, or even harsh— but it is worth it.

I read these verses, and the calling, promise, and game plan that God laid out for Joshua, and I see it as a pattern for my own parenting. He gives the call: Lead them, and lead them well. Graciously, He doesn't stop there; He carries us forward with a sound promise: I will pave the way. And then He doesn't leave us hanging. No, He provides us with the game plan: *Stay in my Word, My Word is truth, and it will guide you forward each step of the way, until this calling is fulfilled*. It is this Word of Truth that gives us all the courage we need to continue moving forward, to take that next right step no matter the fears encroaching around us.

The wicked flee though no one pursues, but the righteous are bold as a lion. (Proverbs 28:1)

Bold as a lion—this is what we must be in order to guide and train our children up in a way that looks much different from our world's way of parenting today. In a culture that has succumbed to passive parenting, it takes great strength and courage to do things differently at the expense of looking authoritarian, strict, or even harsh—but it is worth it. All it takes is looking down the road, to when that glass jar is empty, and picturing your child as a grown, mature, respectable, God-fearing adult—one who still holds a strong relationship with you. It takes courage to walk that road, but as parents, this is the Promised Land that God has called us to.

"Be strong and courageous" (Joshua 1:6).

"Be strong and very courageous" (Joshua 1:7).

"Have I not commanded you? Be strong and courageous" (Joshua 1:9).

Three times God gives the command. The Lord speaks it, but was Joshua really hearing it? Was his heart too submerged in grief and wrought with uncertainty to move forward, or was his heart willing to listen?

Are our hearts ready to hear it?

It wasn't the first time Joshua had been given this command wrapped up in promise. The Lord had spoken these words to Moses before his death. Upon telling Moses that he would soon be laid in the ground, and instructing that Joshua would take his place to see God's purpose fulfilled, the Lord spoke these words to Moses, and commanded him to pass them on to Joshua:

> Then Moses summoned Joshua and said to him in the presence of all Israel, "Be strong and courageous. . . . The Lord himself goes before you and will be with you; he will never leave you nor forsake you. Do not be afraid."
>
> Deuteronomy 31:7–8

Courage was the legacy that Moses passed on to Joshua. And our children need the same kind of legacy. God was preparing Joshua's heart for this grand mission. He is preparing our own hearts for this magnificent mission of parenthood—this great calling He has placed upon us to train our children in His love and Truth.

Fear abounds; uncertainty threatens to capture and deem us helpless to move forward, unable to take a step—but then God's Word returns to our minds, and He whispers gently, "Be strong and courageous. . . . It is the Lord who goes before you." He is a penny ahead of us. He sees that whole jar spent, and then looks at our longing hearts, so desperate to spend them well, and He guides, graciously and beautifully, as we allow Him to go before us and lead.

Joshua must have been prone to fear. Aren't we all, especially when it comes to the well-being of our children? God knew it would not be enough for Joshua to hear this command and promise from the mouth of Moses. Time came for his commissioning. Here Joshua's ears take in the words direct from God's mouth—God in cloud-pillar form. Aged and dying Moses stood beside him, and God spoke it: "Be strong and courageous, for you shall bring the people of Israel into the land that I swore to give them. I will be with you." His heart takes in those words now in first-person form—direct, sharp, pointed, from the very mouth of almighty God—*I will be with you.*

God still speaks those words today.

For all He commands us to, He will be with us. He goes before us. As we nuzzle those swaddled newborns, as we wave good-bye to them when they board the school bus for the very first time, as we send them off to their first slumber party, as we take them for their driver's test, as we wait up for them after their first date, and as tears slip down our face as we kiss them good-bye to college—God is with us. For every moment. For every penny. For every part of this fragile, delicate, beautiful, magnificent mission—He is with us, walking before us, guiding us in that next best step, and leveling the path before us. He is here for it all, and He is faithful to lead us into the Promised Land of a full, abundant life and legacy, one penny at a time.

Questions to Reflect On

- What unknown areas of parenthood are gripping you with fear or anxiety? Who or what could shed light on those unknowns? Begin pursuing that knowledge in prayer, trusting God to give you wisdom and peace for the journey.

- Are you questioning the season or place that God has you in right now? Are you struggling to believe in His best plan for your family? Go to Him with your doubts and questions. He is merciful toward our unbelief, and wants to meet you right where you are.

- Is your heart ready to embrace the command "Be strong and courageous"? Are you ready to steep yourself in the wisdom of His Word for the journey ahead?

-eight-
Preserving
Time

Stones and Gems

"Do you have any collections, Hammy?" With meticulous agility, he moved his little body from rock to rock as we made our way down the riverbed. The evening before, when we had picked my mom up from the airport, he counted it of utmost importance to tell her first of his two collections. "I have a roots collection. And I have a dead-bug collection. It has three bees in it." Now, as we skipped stones and counted ducks along the river, he asked his grandma of her own collections. She thought for a few long moments, suspense hanging in the air as he awaited her answer.

"I like to collect seeds from my plants," she told him. I could picture her bending low to gather seeds in one of her many gardens. I could see the large rubber tires she had spray-painted in bright colors and turned into raised beds.

My boy keeps his collections in a place of honor on his desk, mason jars displaying bugs and plants that have caught his fancy. Once in a while he asks me about my own collection jars. Masons sitting side-by-side on a shelf for us to see often and consider their copper contents. "The pennies help us to remember to spend our time with you well," I explain to him. My heart rests at that, knowing that one day he will understand, when he cradles his own babe for the first time. One day he'll understand that it's not about a jar of pennies, but rather a collection of memories. Each one marking how we've spent time, whether we've invested it in memory-making endeavors.

I want to give my children a storehouse of "Hey, remember when . . . !" moments that will bring a smile to their faces and hope to their hearts years from now, memories to anchor them when the seas of life swell with wild waves.

Parents face this overwhelming pressure to make every moment matter, to cherish every second of this journey. But I don't believe that this idea correctly portrays our calling. I don't think our job is to make every moment memorable. Rather, I believe that our job is to open our eyes wide and sink our feet deep down into those moments when we spot them.

Instead of fabricating and trying to control the memory making, we simply utilize the beauty all around us to cement lasting memories. When those opportunities avail themselves, we are ready and eager to snatch them up and hold them with awe. We'll be ready to turn them into dog ears in the story of our sons' and daughters' childhoods. When she interrupts your work and asks you to push her on the swing, or he insists that you come and see his latest block-tower construction, or she asks for your opinion on a situation with her friends at school—these are gem moments. They shine brightly out from among the ordinary of life, but only if we offer them the attention they are due. They become beacons of light only when we choose to pick them up from among the rocks, polish them with our affection, and set them in a place of honor by naming them as significant. This is when the ordinary transforms from overlooked to holy.

I have a few of these gem moments displayed on my writing desk between half-finished writing projects, half-read books, and art projects from our boys. One is from that day at the duck pond when Zeke taught my mom how to rock hop and asked her about her own collections. They are stones we've collected from our explorations. To anyone else, they might look ordinary, but I know them to be gems. They have been carefully chosen from among thousands like them and then given dignitary treatment. They're rinsed in the river, marked by permanent marker with a date and a memory—"Hike with Zeke," "From Ellis on Devil's Backbone

Hike," "Duck Pond with Mom"—and then set in a place of tribute on my desk. Thrown back into the river, they would be just another stone. Yet sitting on my desk, they serve as a collection of memories, ones that stand out along my motherhood journey as those gem moments to carry me through the difficult days and remind me exactly what this job is about.

I guess it is a little bit like what the Israelites did after God delivered them across the Jordan River. As they stepped to the edge of the river, the waters "which were flowing down from above stood and rose up in one heap. . . . the priests who carried the ark of the covenant of the Lord stood firm on dry ground in the middle of the Jordan while all Israel crossed on dry ground, until all the nation had finished crossing the Jordan" (Joshua 3:16–17 NASB). The nation of Israel did not simply continue on its way after this miraculous crossing. I wonder, though, if that was their instinct. We are told that God spoke to Joshua and instructed him to gather the people and set up Memorial Stones. It makes me wonder if their inclination was to simply keep going. They had places to be, after all. But the Lord stopped them and told them to sink their feet deep into the magnitude of this moment and set up something physical to remind them of what had taken place. "Let this be a sign among you," Joshua instructed the people as they gathered stones, "so that when your children ask later, saying, 'What do these stones mean to you?' then you shall say to them . . ." Their stones were meant to spur on conversation about God's faithfulness.

I want those kinds of Memorial Stones in my own life, so when my children ask about a certain stone on my desk or photo on our wall, I can tell them all about God's faithfulness and beauty toward us woven throughout every moment of our days. And I believe that our penny jars can serve as the same type of physical reminders. Each week as we deposit one penny into the "spent" jar, may it serve as a reminder of God's faithfulness to us throughout that week. And when those pennies are all spent, may our children be able to look at that jar and see memories marked by God's presence and our attention.

Chapters

We were deep in Sunday Morning Rush Mode to get ourselves and all three boys out the door in time for church. Everyone was bathed, fed, and nearly dressed. I was on autopilot, throwing water cups, snacks, and diapers into our bag. That's when I turned and caught a glimpse of our oldest boy—and everything stopped. It felt as though time itself stopped. The tick of the clock ceased to remind me that church would be starting soon and we had to be on our way. Instead, I took in the sight of his shoulders in that button-up. When had they turned from such preschool round to little-boy square? His legs looked impossibly long in those dark denim jeans. And as he ran and jumped throughout the living room, his muscles flexed beneath his Sunday best to reveal a budding strength. A young-man strength. I bent down and rested a knee on the carpet, and pulled him near. "Just stay," I told him. "I just want to hold you for a minute."

He leaned back just enough to catch my eyes with his, and then broke into a big grin. I felt his thin, muscular frame within my embrace. Normally, I would be prone to wonder how this happened. When did my little boy go from seven pounds four ounces to this young man? Except I was learning, by God's grace, how it happens: I had been paying attention. I knew how those shoulders had squared and those calf muscles had rounded and that jaw had taken shape, because I was watching when he scaled the tree in the backyard, or took off full speed down a hiking trail. I was there, because I am beginning to see that I cannot miss those moments for the world. I want so badly to see the process, not only the end result. I fear getting to the end only to look back and wonder how we got there. I want to look back and see evidence of our carefully chosen steps. I want to see a trail of picnic afternoons and stargazing and marshmallow-rimmed smiles around the campfire. I want to be all there, so that when we look back, we'll know just how we got here.

Parenthood gives little thought to our emotions or agendas as it ticks our days away. Perhaps you felt it the first time you stroked those impossibly tiny toes and fingers, still pink and raisin-like, new from the womb. Or maybe when you watched your child take his first steps, or heard her tell you she loved you for the very first time. It is this impossible pull, a tension within our souls, rejoicing over every new milestone while mourning the loss required to reach that new step. As one chapter opens, one must close. And the closing of those chapters is at times too much for our hearts to bear.

One day we look at our child only to realize that they haven't said a certain word in a certain way, or asked for that blanket they used to require for bedtime, or worn those footie pajamas they used to refuse to take off, or asked us to hold their hand over the foot bridge. Our spirits inhale and exhale with a constant mourning and rejoicing, this forward motion that time demands and we cannot control. We develop this great longing to slow time, to capture it so that this moment, this experience, can never escape our grasp. We worry that our memory won't be enough. That it won't recall his tiny voice, her soft cheeks, those dimples when he giggles. *Will we remember?* The truth of it is this: We will only remember those moments in all of their brilliant detail to the extent that we pay attention now. If we succumb to distraction, failing to memorize the details now, then we choose to never see those details again. They will escape us if we are not careful.

This has been my experience in motherhood. I watch my children as they grow and learn and change so quickly before my eyes, trying desperately to remember just how they looked, how they loved, who they were only months ago. And in that striving,

I realize that there is so much I forget, so much that time won't allow me to hold on to.

Author Ann Kroeker writes of drawing these moments into deep memory:

> When my son called a pancake a "pampake," I laughed, mussed his hair, and then lifted him out of his booster chair to change his diaper so I could run an errand. I remembered it because I retold the story to a friend later that same day. Plus, he said "pampake" for a long time before he straightened it out. But I wonder how many of those sweet moments have been lost to me because I did not draw them deep into memory.[1]

There is this ache so deep within us to never surrender one of those precious details of who our child is at every stage. We want to know the newborn-them, the infant-them, the toddler-them, the preschool-them, the child-them, and the adolescent-them all at once. But at this moment we have the now-them. And are we getting to know them the best we can? That way, when they close this chapter and we walk together into the next, we'll know what steps it took to get there. We'll be well acquainted with the journey that is a part of them, and a part of us. We'll remember, and we'll be better prepared for the next chapter when the clock chimes in its arrival.

As we kiss them good-night, we know they will not be the same tomorrow as they were today. As they unfold into their older, more mature selves, we receive the great gift of being a front-row witness to this development, but it leaves a great void, a feeling of loss, as we must let go of what was. This is why we, as moms and dads, must always practice the art of capturing time with our full attention—and bottling it up for safekeeping once all of our pennies are spent.

From Humdrum to Holy

It is something like a dream, those first days home with a newborn baby: a bit hazy—mostly from sleep deprivation—but altogether magical. There is something glorious about the scent of a newborn and friends showing up at your doorstep with warm meals. But then one day we wake up after another sleep-deprived night, and it's kind of old news. *We are kind of old news.* And although the beauty of it all is still there, life begins to adopt a new sense of normalcy.

The laundry sits untouched. Countless onesies bought with such attention and care months ago now sit heaped in a pile smelling of spit-up, begging for some laundry detergent and stain remover. This new normal develops with each load of dishes needing to be washed, with each middle-of-the-night feeding, with each quick kiss to the spouse before they leave for work, with every day that our own hair goes unbrushed and as pajamas become the expected attire from wake-up until final exhausted laying down to sleep— until the baby awakes to be fed, of course.

All at once it seems that life is composed of the mundane, and we grow weary of the sameness, the repetition, the seeming insignificance of it all. One parent grabs their cup of now-cold coffee and heads off to work while the other tries to make sense of what needs to be cleaned first and tries to remember the last time the baby was changed. And somewhere in the mess and the exhaustion of it all, we feel like we are losing ourselves. Yet this losing of ourselves is a necessary part of becoming the parents our children need us to be. This losing ourselves—we must come to a point when we embrace it and transform it into a giving up of ourselves instead. A giving away of all we have to offer for the sake of our marriages, our children's upbringing and futures, and our family legacy.

It is in the humdrum ordinary of parenthood that we uncover the holiness of parenthood. The holy mundane that ebbs and flows through those piles of laundry, the sameness of days, and the fatigue of it all. All of it—every bit—is all the holy work of God. Author Lisa-Jo Baker calls it

> a gift from God who names every part of who we are and what we do significant. Because, "He is before all things, and in Him *all things hold together.*" There is no part of our everyday, wash-and-repeat routine of kids and laundry and life and fights and worries and playdates and aching budgets and preschool orientations and work and marriage and love and new life and bedtime marathons that Jesus doesn't look deep into and say, "That is Mine." In Him *all* things hold together.[2]

When the clock strikes bedtime and my son calls from his room asking for one more drink of water, or to go potty just one last time, or for two wet wipes to sleep with—not one, but two—or for that one specific red car that he happened to leave out buried in the dirt of our backyard that he now requires in order to fall asleep, there is so much holy wrapped up in the whole of it all. It is the shepherding, the development of our own patience, the guiding and navigating of these littles ones from birth on. It is a holy calling. And not only when we curl up for a Bible story and share the gospel with them, or take them to church, or teach them the importance of generosity. There is holiness found in every nook and cranny of parenthood. Every prayer, every opportunity for grace, every toy picked up, every playdate at the park, every sit-down over homework and cookies—God looks down on it all and says, "This is good." And so we can, too.

Sometimes I stop right in the middle of the dust bunnies, thin-stretched budget, sleepless nights, smudged windows, and quarrels over Matchbox cars; I stop and step back and see it—this blessed life. With beauty dripping off the edges of every little imperfect piece of our days. And right there in the middle of the mess I find the miracle that I get to walk through these days with them by my side. Those moments, when I can look past the mess and the noise and the questions and the pressures to see beyond them and into the beauty that is us together, those are the clearest moments for me. They're unadulterated by my false notions of perfect and self-imposed pressures. Those moments, when I can sit and laugh and play and just be there next to my child, I catch a glimpse of God's design for parenthood.

> Every prayer, every opportunity for grace, every toy picked up, every playdate at the park, every sit-down over homework and cookies— God looks down on it all and says, "This is good." And so we can, too.

It is this breathtaking scene, much like when God walked side-by-side with Adam and Eve in the garden, when we understand the glory and healing and life that there is in the simple gift of connection. We were designed for it. Our children were crafted for it. And although it can seem like the most ordinary of things—to sit on the floor and craft a tower out of blocks, or engage in a game of hide-and-seek, or pull out a board game—it is actually one of the greatest ways that we can fulfill our calling. And when we do this, the humdrum, insignificant pieces of our days take on a whole new look.

Oftentimes as my boys climb into bed at night and I tuck them in, I ask them what their favorite part of the day was. They think for a moment before their eyes light up. I can almost see the memory dancing in their minds as a smile creeps across their face. "Coloring with you!" they'll reply, or, "Building a tent!" Their answers are laced with simplicity. But then, when I look back on our day, I often see that those were my favorite parts of it, too, those moments when I chose to stop chasing after perfection and grandeur and productivity, and instead to embrace the humdrum and transform it into something holy and lasting. That is the power of our presence in their days. And this is when moments transform from fleeting blips of time to memories worth preserving.

Cemeteries and Stream Beds

There is a small hidden cemetery that sits on the outskirts of the town where I was raised in Wisconsin. I don't recall where my mom was on this day. Perhaps having lunch with a friend. And I couldn't tell you why my dad took us three kids out to that spot. But it was not at all unlike him to surprise us with the unordinary. He pulled the car off onto a small gravel patch in front of an old brick building. My sister, brother, and I piled out of the car and made our way around the building, where we walked on a wet, dewy grass path along a horse pasture. The horses lifted their heads, chewing grass as they nodded to us. As we walked, trees began to frame us in on both sides, arching overtop of us to create a beautiful green canopy, we kids still unsure of where this natural awning was ushering us.

Finally we reached a worn wrought-iron gate dressed in vines of ivy. We stepped around the gate and began exploring the lush, green expanse of land. We made our way around aged gravestones, reading names and dates and wondering about stories. My dad told us folk tales, at one point looking through his binoculars to a gravestone on the far side of the cemetery. "Quiet," he whispered, ducking us close behind a fallen tree. "Did you see that?" We didn't blink. He handed the binoculars to my brother. Ian took hold of them, placed them to his eyes, and looked hard.

"No." He looked on for a few moments before he finally caught on to my dad's wink, my sister and I wholly unaware of their stunt. Our hearts beat hard within our chests. No one spoke for a few moments, and then, "Hurry, run!" My dad exclaimed it loudly as he ushered us quickly back toward the cemetery entrance. We made it halfway back to that wrought-iron gate before he and my brother erupted in laughter and my sister and I remembered to breathe before shooting them unamused glances, followed by some giggles of our own.

Looking back on that day, the joke could have seemed a bit heartless from the outside looking in, yet it was anything but. The whole adventure—from pulling onto that gravel drive, to the horses bidding us hello, to the mystery that hovered in the air as we walked through that canopy of trees, to the names and stories on those headstones, and finally to the thrill of my dad's imagination—it was all so unexpected, mysterious, and fanciful. Which is why it has stuck with me all these years later. Surprise has that way about it. When we give our child the gift of an unexpected adventure, not only do they sense our thought and intention behind it, but the thrill of it has a way of sealing that time into their memory bank.

After that day, I would return to that little cemetery often. I would have my prom photos taken among the spring flowers and worn headstones. And years later, I would bring my boyfriend to that magical place that had left a special mark on my childhood. We'd snap a black-and-white photo of us stealing a kiss from each other between those worn headstones. We'd use that photo a year later on our wedding invitations. For years following that day that my dad took us to the cemetery, I would find solace in these places. I would pack my Bible and journal and spend hours in the quiet retreats among the headstones, soaking in silence and pondering legacies. I found peace in those places, and I believe it all began back on that day when my dad chose to use a few hours to take his children on an unlikely adventure, one so out of our ordinary that it immediately cemented itself as an important memory. One that would stand the test of time.

I have come to see over the years, looking back on my own upbringing and now watching my own boys' childhoods unfold, that the strongest of memories can be made when we step out of our ordinary. When we leave behind routine and break away from the expected. When we take that step outside of what our children expect, it sends them an immediate signal: *Wait, pay attention, this is going to be special!* All of their attention turns to you and the new agenda, or lack thereof, and their minds begin the process of etching this special time into their spirits, somewhere to be kept safe for decades to come.

I'm not sure why stepping outside of routine can be so difficult for some of us, myself included. What I do know, however, is that some of my favorite memories with my husband and boys are the ones we made when we decided to ditch our agenda and go in search of something beautiful, fun, and well worth our time. Whether it's picking your child up early from school to go on a nature hike or, as my parents did on occasion, telling us we were going to an antique mall and instead pulling into the movie theater parking lot or the water park. As soon as we caught on, we could see that our parents had us and adventure in mind, and that this was going to be a day to remember. The adventure itself need not be something extraordinary in nature. It becomes remarkable, rather, in its unexpected arrival in our day.

> When we take that step outside of what our children expect, it sends them an immediate signal: **Wait, pay attention, this is going to be special!**

It happened one day with my own kids, when my afternoon was blocked out for catching up on work. As we dressed the boys for church, my mind was already racing toward productivity mode, readying itself for attacking my to-do list as soon as church let out. But then my husband suggested a picnic in the mountains. Immediately I felt the tension in both my heart and my neck. It has become very difficult for me to say no to propositions such as that. However, it is equally difficult for me to switch my mind from work-mode to play-mode. When I have my mind set on getting things done, to give that up feels like a failure. But on that day, I chose play. I put out of my head any notions of getting work done, and we packed the cooler up and set out for the mountains. That afternoon ended up being one that I will never forget.

The sky was a clear, indigo blue, and it poured its bright color straight into the stream that my husband, boys, and I walked in between towering mountain peaks. I laid my sweater down on the bed of sand and gravel next to the stream and sat down to watch. The water was perfect, and our boys laughed with pure delight as they ran and splashed and spotted minnows swimming between their feet. As I observed them fully feeling, seeing, smelling, and taking in the wonder around us, no detail was lost on me: the way our toddler walked apprehensively through the tall grass, unsure of the sensation of it brushing against his skin; the way my husband waded through the mountain stream, eyes locked on the world just beneath the surface, in search of brook trout; the way our boys would glance back at me every few minutes, mountain peaks, aspens, and wonder reflected in their eyes. And to think, none of it would have taken place if we had not chosen on that day to lay aside our agendas, trading them for an adventure that years from now can stand in our children's memories as a remarkable piece of their childhood—a penny very well spent—just as I look back on that day my dad took my brother, sister, and me on an unlikely adventure to that small, hidden cemetery.

The Gift
of Their Own Stories

After several years of sharing my family's story on my blog, I began to sense that there was something behind that blog more powerful than I had realized. I thought that I had been writing for my small following of readers and for myself, to help me better understand our story. But I was beginning to see that I was also writing for my sons. Every time I hit "publish" on a blog post, I was preserving a part of their story. And years from now, when they are grown, they will have this vault of memories filled from their childhood. And the greatest piece of this gift to them is that these stories are written from their mother's perspective. They will have this glimpse into what I was thinking, dreaming, struggling through, and praying for during these years of raising them.

Whether we have experience in writing or not, whether we enjoy it or not, we as parents have an opportunity to document our kids' childhoods from our own perspective. I can only imagine what joy your son or daughter will find in reading exactly what you, their mom or dad, were feeling the first time they took a step, boarded a school bus, drove a car, or headed off to college. What a gift, when they are adults with a whole new depth of understanding, to read how you struggled through deciding on a preschool for them, or how you felt the first time they left for a week at summer camp. And when they are new parents, navigating those deep waters of sleep deprivation and endless anxieties over raising a child, what a gift for them to be able to read and recognize the very same thoughts and feelings that you were having when you brought them home from the hospital or orphanage.

I have kept journals for each of my boys ever since I saw those faint pink lines on the pregnancy tests. In these journals I don't normally record their weight, height, or even many milestones met. Instead, I record their musings, what makes them tick, something they said during the day that gave me a clearer glimpse into who they are. You don't need to have a creative writing degree or successful blog. You only need a pen, a notebook, and your full attention.

On occasion I glance back through the journals, and that is when I see it—a jar full. Nine hundred and thirty-six pennies rich. And the photos, the voices, the words, the memories of each week, each day, each moment from the maternity ward until now, I see them well spent. Even in those seasons when I feel like I'm just not getting things right, when I feel as though my patience is short and my attention is split, and I doubt myself as their mother, these stories and memories inscribed by ink offer me a glimpse of a bigger picture. And I know that they will do the same for my boys someday. Through those words written by the hand of their mom, they'll witness the traces of God's grace weaving its way throughout their stories. They'll see my own imperfections, failures, and fears, as well as the overcoming, the victory, and the triumphs.

It has been difficult to keep up this practice. It takes time to sit down and put a pen to paper. And yet, whenever and however we do it—by writing or typing or picture-taking or scrapbooking— the preservation of their memories and our perspective on raising them is a unique gift that only we can give them. Knowing that, I carve out time to sit down with those journals again, or I snap a few photos of the ordinary moments of our day, and I place them somewhere for safekeeping, so that one day when our pennies are spent, they can look back and know exactly what I was thinking in that moment.

Photos are one of my favorite ways of preserving time. And yet, it's a difficult balance, this memory-preserving and life-living all at the same time. There have been seasons of my motherhood when I've let the camera come between me and the memories themselves. Desperate to capture a moment, I miss the moment entirely. Sometimes, for the moment to have opportunity to become a memory, we have to set the camera down. I realized this one evening while we were on a family vacation.

The sun was about to dip below the horizon, and its light had already receded from the woods. I had only to round a corner and run down our road to get back to the cabin we were renting. But then . . . *is that real?* I stopped in my tracks, feet frozen in place. The huge animal looked like a statue. *Was it there when I had left earlier for my run?* I slowly began backing away. She didn't move. There was no one else around. Then, finally, I heard gravel crunching behind me as the headlights from a car illuminated the street. I waved to the woman driving. She slowed her car and rolled down her window. The dog in her lap greeted me excitedly.

> It's a difficult balance, this memory-preserving and life-living all at the same time. . . . Sometimes for the moment to have opportunity to become a memory, we have to set the camera down.

"I'm so sorry . . ." I wondered if I seemed like a crazy person, out here alone in the dark, still sweating and panting from my run, and now about to explain that I can't figure out whether or not this massive animal is real. But then I glanced over, and her head was low to the ground, where it hadn't been before. She was real.

"It's just that there's a very large moose right over there, and I am kind of terrified of running past her." The woman motioned to the passenger side of her car. "Oh, well, get in!" she exclaimed. What would have normally been very uncharacteristic of me—to hop into a stranger's car—seemed quite normal up here in the wild, where one must depend on another for safety. I lowered myself into her car and reached for my phone to record the moment. That's when the screen went black. "My word, my batteries just died."

She drove slowly, stopping so we could admire the animal. "Is that a baby?" It was. Actually, there were three. I had only seen a few moose since our move to the mountains six months prior, but never a baby. The mother glanced up at us between bites of foliage, keeping her kin safely tucked between her and the trees. Minutes later the kind stranger, Barb, dropped me off at the driveway of the cabin we were staying at that week. I thanked her again, then went inside to tell my husband of my adventure, but without a photo of the majestic creatures that had interrupted my run. Detailing to him their beauty, and the fear I felt in the moment I saw her, I found myself thankful that I didn't have a photo, because some experiences in life are meant to be captured only by the spirit, not by the camera.

Perhaps some of your moments will transform into even richer memories when you choose to set down the camera and instead write about the moment, recalling all the vivid details and taking the time to inscribe them on paper or retell them in all their color and glory to your spouse, child, or friend.

When we set down the camera, we can grasp that moment in its right-here, only-now beauty. Without a device between us and the happening, we can take in every single detail. This is why, whether I am at the playground spinning the boys on the tire swing or we're bending low in the woods to inspect a mushroom clinging to a fallen tree, I often and deliberately put my phone away. For me, this has been a difficult practice to come by. I love images and video. From a very young age, when my father introduced me to photography, I have been intrigued with capturing time and preserving it through photos.

I hate the thought of letting a magical moment slip by. But sometimes the magic is found precisely in the one-time-only nature of it. I feel it when I am sitting next to a lake, my youngest snacking on a granola bar as he sits in my lap watching the waves. His big brother climbs the rocks behind him. The camera is put away, and this moment will always and forever be only ours. I can tell it in story, but the colors and beauty of it all, that is mine, safely tucked within my heart for when I most need to remember what truly matters in life. Many times we can give something or someone our full attention only when we set the camera down. And only then does that moment bloom into the fullest memory it was meant to be, safely tucked away in the hearts of those who were there to experience it.

Handing Over a Legacy

Some parents have told me that they plan on passing on their jar of 936 pennies to their child when they are grown and moving away. It is a stunning visual, the handing off of time well invested—the giving away of each moment to the child, now grown. Those pennies, how much more they will mean when your grown child can glance into that transparent glass and recall with vivid memory how they were spent and invested throughout their childhood.

I want those pennies, when my sons look at them, to bring back to mind afternoon picnics at the park, hikes along mountain streams, evenings spent cuddled up in my lap amidst a pile of books, and the time we skipped church on Easter morning (I know . . .) to have an entire day at the Omaha Zoo. I want them to glimpse that jar, one that speaks of time slowed down, amplified, and made full. I am sure that you wish for the same. Give those pennies great meaning in your child's heart. We can do this, but only by treasuring up the memories we are making right now, storing them inside those pennies, and passing them on with vivid clarity. It is in the preservation of those memories—yes, in the initial making of them, and then the capturing through words and photos, and the retelling of them through the years—that those pennies gain meaning that will bless and guide your child for the remainder of their lifetime. When we capture those memories, we possess a gift that only we can give them—their childhood from our personal perspective.

As children, they can't see the ins and outs of all of their behaviors, passions, responses, and characteristics—they are blinded to so much of themselves that only we, as their parents, can see. Children often cannot remember far enough back, or vividly enough, to pick apart their childhood or the lessons it holds for them now. But we can capture all of that for them.

Some of the parents who said they would be passing on their jars, they also told me of how they were keeping journals for each of their children, which they also plan on passing along with the jars. When it comes time each week to deposit one penny into the "spent" jar, they stop to journal a few things from the week— how exactly that penny was invested. Just consider how powerful that will be for

> When we capture those memories, we possess a gift that only we can give them—their childhood from our personal perspective.

their children to read years from now, to behold those pennies and then read exact and specific ways that they were intentionally invested by their parents. Make that glass jar a gift you are proud to pass on—one that will mean the world to your child because they understand what those pennies were made of.

One early fall day, the mailman came to our door. He only brings the mail directly to our door when he has a package to deliver, and so I rose with anticipation. He delivered a bright orange flat package into my hands, and immediately I knew what it was. My heart began to beat faster. I thanked him politely, closed the door, and turned back toward my husband, who was sitting on the couch. "What's that?" he asked me quizzically. Perhaps he sensed my jittering heart. "It's for you." I made a fast decision to give it to him straightaway. I had planned on waiting, perhaps for the perfect moment on some date night to hand him this gift I'd been crafting for him over the past month. But now, with the boys fast asleep for their naps, now was as good a time as any. As he pulled back the tape on the package from an online photo book company, my heart continued to flutter—I had poured so much of my soul into this project for him, all without his knowing.

He opened the package and ran his fingers over the smooth cover of the book. "I've seen this picture before," he commented. On the cover was a photo I had taken of our son in the weeks after our move to Kansas City. You couldn't see his face, but you could see his tiny hands and feet, blurred from motion, climbing the staircase to the apartment we had stayed in before we found our home. Under the photo read this quote from Martin Luther King Jr.: "Take the first step in faith. You don't have to see the whole staircase, just take the first step." That photo, and that quote, encapsulated my emotions and convictions around the move we had made one year ago—a move surrounded by such immense uncertainty but defined by a fierce faith God had placed within our hearts.

My husband gently opened the book, revealing photos from the year before. Each page told a story of our recent move—through photos, quotes, Scriptures, excerpts from the stories on my blog, and thoughts from my journal. It was a recollection of the most arduous and most beautiful year of our life so far. His eyes became glossy as he took in our year as a whole.

Pictures and words are powerful agents of memory preservation. You don't have to be an artist to employ them. I didn't always take pictures, and I didn't always write stories. But when we began our family, I was so desperate for a way to hold on to these moments, to grasp them in such a way as to graft them into my very being, to make them a part of me that I could pass on to my children and their children.

Preserving memories does not need to be an elaborate display of art. It does not mean that you have to spend hours hunched over scrapbooking materials—unless, of course, you want to! There are cheap services that take photos straight off your phone and send you a printed book with no work on your end! A good friend of mine has this set up to automatically send her a book of her own photos every few months. It can be as easy as keeping a small notebook in your diaper bag or purse and jotting down little things that your children say throughout your days. These little acts of capturing moments all add up to a legacy packed full of life lived side by side.

These memories are the very threads of the legacy we hand off when each of those 936 pennies are all spent up. This legacy crafting is our job now. It is done moment by moment, right in the middle of overwhelmed budgets, overfilled laundry baskets, and overstacked dirty dishes. Right here, right now in this moment, is opportunity for that penny this week. And each time we choose play and love and laughter over stress and guilt and shame, we fill that jar full of significance. And one day, whether we physically hand that jar off to our child or not, it will make all the difference—how we are spending our time right now, today. Tomorrow does not build a legacy. Today does.

Questions to Reflect On

- What physical reminder could you set up in your home to honor the gem moments in life? Stones from hikes and adventures? A photo book of memories? A simple list on the fridge of favorite family quotes? Begin preserving memories this week.

- What are two ways this week that you can transform a humdrum routine into a holy moment and lasting memory?

- How can you step outside of the ordinary and expected this week and offer your child a surprise adventure to seal into their memory vault?

-nine-

Buying
Back Time

Reclaiming 205 Pennies

He asked the question in his soft, sweet voice. He even added a "please" at the end. Everything I had taught him about asking nicely, he did. And then he stood, looking up into my eyes, awaiting my response. My resolve wavered on the edge of the decision I had made the day before. And then I looked back into those sweet blue eyes . . . and told him *no*. Guilt moved in quickly and settled on my shoulders. Who tells their child *no* to such a simple request on their birthday? Birthdays are usually *yes* days. *Yes*, you can have another piece of cake. *Yes*, we can go to your favorite park. *Yes*, we can have your favorite meal for dinner. And yet here I was, telling him *no*.

His birthday fell in the weeks following a bigger decision that had been made, one to protect our family. It was brave and bold and proving itself hard, especially now, as I looked into my boy's eyes. My husband and I had recently made the decision to transition our kids and ourselves away from the dependency on screens and media that we had slipped into. Our oldest was waking earlier in the mornings and forgoing any nap. Suddenly there were three additional hours to his day—and mine—that we needed to fill. TV had become a huge part of that filler, my default for keeping him occupied. Conviction was pulling at my heart every day as I pressed "Play next episode" and watched my boy transfixed on the pixels dancing across the TV. I knew that his days were meant for more.

It was not that we were against allowing our children to watch TV. It was that I was coming to realize that the TV was becoming my default go-to, and the boys were adopting an attitude of entitlement toward it. They were beginning to see TV as an everyday event and integral part of their day. And we were not okay with that.

As I usually do when it comes to tough decisions and life changes like these, I decided to blog about our journey as a way of keeping myself accountable. I spent a morning out at my favorite coffee shop, writing and journaling about the decision. And as I did, I dove back into some research that I had begun a year and a half earlier. What I found left me heartbroken and more determined than ever to release my sons from the grip of technology. I wanted to prepare them to live their lives fully, despite our culture's dependency on media and entertainment.

Today's child, from when they are born until they turn eighteen, spends roughly an average of 205 waking weeks staring at a screen.[1] Two hundred and five *waking weeks*! I picture those penny jars on our shelf, and I imagine myself removing nearly one fourth of those pennies and throwing them directly into the trash can. It is heart-wrenching. My heart ached with regret over my own decisions, and it despaired for the futures of kids across our world. I mourned the loss of countless childhoods and broken families. Of course, screen time is not the only contributor to these travesties, but I was beginning to glimpse just how big a part it is playing in dividing families and distracting kids from a life that really matters.

These were the very things that were threading together the cord of our decision into a strong and lasting resolve. Within my heart began to burn an anger toward what I was seeing and how it threatened my family. I was ready to fight back, which is why I told my son *no* on his birthday. I want more for my boys than what today's society is offering them. I'm sure you feel the same for your own children. There is a battle before us parents. It is a daunting one, but we have the power to fight it. We have the final say. And we do have what it takes to offer our children a life built on strong childhood memories and the ingredients of a life that truly matters.

That morning I gently told my boy *no*, that we weren't going to watch TV, and suggested that he play outside instead. This answer is not always met with instant obedience. In the days prior, there had been whining and pouting. But today was different. I realized that we were turning a corner when he immediately ran outside and strapped on his bike helmet. That is when I began to glimpse the hope that parents have in this battle. Throughout my research and writing, I kept coming back to this one thought. When it comes to screen time, parents face a lot of guilt. People are always saying that kids should watch less TV, play fewer video games, and spend less time on social media. Yet we feel powerless. Parents, *we are not powerless*. And what we need now is not guilt, but hope.

Gary Chapman, in a book he coauthored with Arlene Pellicane entitled *Growing Up Social*, offers some of this hope when he writes, "It takes effort to switch from the convenience of screen time to an interactive or tactile activity for a child. But the benefits for your son's or daughter's development are well worth it. You will be pleasantly surprised at how quickly your child adjusts to new screen-free routines."[2]

In the weeks that followed our decision, this is exactly what I saw. At the outset, the mission seemed daunting. The will of a three-year-old is strong, after all, and I knew that tantrums dotted the path before us. Yet I quickly discovered that this was what my sons had been longing for. As I watched them play

> Kids want to create. It's engrained into the fiber of their beings to imagine, explore, and problem-solve.

for hours in the backyard, climb trees, create off-road tracks for their toy cars, dream, imagine, and create, I witnessed their young spirits thriving. It ends up that kids *want* to create. It's engrained into the fiber of their beings to imagine, explore, and problem-solve. They want to be challenged and to overcome. Their words may speak otherwise at first, but they want to be bored, because boredom often leads to the most grand adventures! Turning off the TV provides space for them to create and embark on those adventures.

I was beginning to see that this battle has not already been won. Yes, we are up against a beast. Really, we are up against society. We as parents have the power and authority to redeem our kids' childhoods, reclaim our legacies, and protect our families. We only need to be brave enough to do things differently. And no matter how far along we are in the journey, or how entrenched in screen-time habits, it's never too late to choose to be brave. It starts with taking a hard look in the mirror.

I am not an anti-technology mom. In fact, I run an online business from our home. My responsibilities for that business, along with writing, demand that I spend a significant amount of time in front of screens. It would be naïve of us as parents to ignore the fact that society is more and more depending upon technology for jobs, and to not prepare our children to succeed in such a world is ignorant. However, success is not only found in teaching them how to use technology; it's also in teaching them the proper balance of technology in their lives.

We do our children a world of good in training them that technology is a tool to be used and not a master over us. It is a constant struggle for me as a writer and business owner to balance my use of technology. It requires boundaries and a constant refocusing on how much, and why, I am using technology. It takes asking myself questions such as:

- Is my use of technology in this moment purposeful?
- Do my kids understand why I am on my laptop right now? Am I communicating to them the importance of my work? Am I including them by letting them into my world of work?
- Am I placing the urgent before the important? Can this wait until the kids are napping or in bed?
- Have I crossed the line from work priority to mindless social media scanning?

Asking these types of questions, and revisiting them often, keeps me grounded and balanced in my use of media. If I am honest, these questions often find me in the wrong place, but they are quick to redirect me back into intentional territory and guide me back into a life that really matters.

What might your own questions be when it comes to checking in on your use of technology? I wonder just how different our families and our society would be today if we parents took on the responsibility of modeling to our kids a proper balance. It is our job to show them by example that face-to-face relationships are more important than the game on the screen. That friends in front of us come before social media. That more often than not, emails and texting can wait. And that eye contact is a rare gem these days, so let's preserve it with all we've got.

I read of one mom who found a creative way to check in on her own technology use, one that went viral around the internet for its profound message. She shared her findings online, and they challenged thousands of parents like us to reconsider the messages we are sending to our children. She performed an experiment in which she set down her phone and quietly observed her two boys. She recorded on a piece of paper every time one of her boys looked at her in search of some kind of response. When they performed a trick and looked to see whether she was watching, or when they looked to her for some sort of approval, she made a mark on her sheet of paper. What she found was that in that short time, her children looked at her twenty-eight times. And what she realized was that on a normal day, she would have been distracted by the phone in her hand. "Twenty-eight times my angels would have wondered if the World Wide Web was more important than them," she wrote. And then she ended her post with a call to action, a plea to fellow parents to set down their phones, to be different, to spend time with loved ones, and to be aware of what their media use is communicating to their children.

The next generation of children is counting on us to teach them how to be adults. When I glance around today at what most adults (including me) spend the bulk of our time staring at, I feel this heavy ache for my children. I want so much more for them. I want them to feel the emotional and spiritual connection that happens in an authentic conversation with another human being. I want them to find comfort, belonging, and assurance in eye contact. I want them to catch the intricate details of the world around them, and not pass them by because they were distracted by what is temporary and fleeting.

To be completely honest, I do not always convey the right messages to my own children. With the lure and power of media in our day and age, we're bound to lose sight of our values at times. That is when we have the opportunity to teach our children another invaluable virtue—apology.

There have been times when I have needed to close my laptop, apologize to my son, and explain to him that he is more important than my work. That is not failure—that is grace. Let's embrace that grace and commit to this lifelong journey of discovering and modeling a proper balance of life and technology. Our children are watching us more than we realize; we hold the power to shape their futures by being aware of the values and priorities we are communicating to them every single day. We cannot afford to throw away 205 pennies from our jars.

What's in
Your Child's Hands?

My oldest boy took my hand in his and gave it two gentle squeezes. In that moment, everything around us became unimportant. It was just him and me, standing there in this blink of time that would imprint itself into the deepest part of me. It seemed that lately he was hanging on to every word I said, and this was proof of that. Two days before, I had squeezed his own little hand in mine. When he had asked me why I did it, I explained, "It's a way to tell someone that you love them without using words. It shows them you are thinking about them." He quickly adopted this into his vocabulary of showing love, surprising me with hand squeezes while we were in the car, out on a walk, and running errands. It serves as a constant reminder that he's thinking about me, his hand memorizing the feeling of my own as he grips it tightly in his own, then lets go and smiles up at me. I'm surprised by how much comfort and security it brings to my own heart.

It is this new practice of his that makes me hyperaware in the weeks to come of what is occupying my boy's hands. When he is not holding on to me, what fills his hands?

In her book *Hands Free Life*, Rachel Macy Stafford writes, "I want my daughters to remember holding our cat, Banjo; a wooden spoon to form cookie dough; musical instruments; books; bike handlebars; ladybugs; seashells; and especially my hand in theirs."[3] When all of our pennies are spent and our weeks are passed and our children are carrying on their new lives, what do we want them to remember filling their hands with as a child? What textures do we want engrained into their memories, and what will the calluses and scars on their fingers be made of?

I want my children to know well the slight cramp of thumb and wrist after gripping a marker or paintbrush, as they splash color across a blank canvas. I want them to know the feeling of both bread dough and garden soil caked under their fingernails. When their hands slip into mine, I want to feel their small calluses from swinging on the monkey bars and pulling each other around the yard in the wagon. I want them to be well acquainted with the feeling of craft glue dried onto the tips of their fingers. I want those same fingertips to know the softness of bird feathers and the prickles of pine needles. I want them to know how to hold a peapod between their hands and slice it open with their thumbnail to get at the peas inside. I want them to memorize the perfect hand placements and how to grip the branches just right to scale the tree at their favorite park. Most of all, I want my children to know the assurance found in the slight squeeze of my hand around theirs, a silent reminder that I love them and am thinking about them right there in that moment—and that I wouldn't rather my hand be busy with anything else.

What our children observe our hands holding day in and day out will greatly determine what they decide to busy their own hands with. By paying a little more attention to what occupies our hands right now, we can shift the trajectory of their childhood, and their future, into more intentional territory. I want my children to see my hands occupied with the pages of a book, a pen, and my journal, or with a tennis ball as I join them out in the backyard for a game of catch. I know that many times—too many times—they see my hands busying themselves in a cadence across the laptop keyboard, or they watch my thumb dancing across the screen of my smartphone. And yes, the work is important, but I have to ask myself: Do they see my hands wrapped around technology more than they see them fingering the pages of a book, sprinkling cinnamon-sugar over muffins, or wrapped around their daddy's hand?

Today, may we all pay a little more attention to what we occupy our hands with, choosing to fill them with the very things we hope our children will wrap their own hands around. May we be the ones to model what is truly important in life by what we choose to grasp within our palms.

I see it when we travel or take a vacation—their hands eager for something new. I look at a photo from a few years back: our oldest boy, then two years old, hands tucked tight into winter gloves as he holds a fishing pole. Next to him sits his uncle; his grandpa's not far outside the frame. My husband was a few feet away taking the photo. They're all huddled together in a small tent, ice-fishing on Lake Superior, where my husband's family lives. That evening we'll all gather around a big table and push Christmas-tree- and star-shaped cutters into soft cookie dough. We'll slather icing on the still-warm cookies, and dash red and white sprinkles across each one. Everyone's hands busy with cookie creating and memory making.

> What our children observe our hands holding day in and day out will greatly determine what they decide to busy their own hands with.

I see it also every Thanksgiving, when my entire side of the family gets together for a whole week. For seven days we watch as my and my sister's kids, five children born within five years' time, busy their hands with crafts, board games, gingerbread-house making, and books. On a chilly afternoon this most recent Thanksgiving, my husband took all five children out to the yard to gather sticks for a fire. My husband, along with all five Little Adventurers, quickly disappeared into the nearby forest. Just as I caught sight of the last straggling hikers disappearing behind the evergreens, I buttoned up my coat, tied on my shoes, and ran up the hill to join their adventure. Thoughts of gathering twigs and branches had moved to the back burner in their young minds. Our five-year-old, Zeke, had discovered a trail, and they were off to see where it would take them. For the next hour, my husband and I hiked that trail along the mountain with our three boys and my niece and nephew. Our black Labrador zigzagged around the children, keeping a watchful eye on each of them. My niece, Hanna, was four years old and not a very experienced hiker. Yet that afternoon, she took charge. I watched in awe as she fearlessly grasped at branches to help her up a steep hillside. When she fell and tumbled a few feet down into some bushes, she hopped up, wiped off her pink winter coat, and continued on her way. When we finally arrived back at the cabin with rosy noses, the kids warmed their hands around mugs of hot chocolate, eagerly awaiting quality time with the coloring pages and colored pencils strewn about the table.

It is afternoons like that, with our hands full of twigs and sticky with sap, that I realize that this could be one of our greatest strategies in spending our time well: Taking note of what is in our hands has a way of helping us check in on what's filling our minds and hearts. When my kids see my hands busy in the garden, or tracing words in my Bible, or wrapped around a good book, it speaks multitudes to them about my priorities, and it helps to shape their own. Every week as we take a penny between our fingers and deposit it into the "spent jar," may it be a reminder to us all to take account of what we're telling our children through what we're holding in our hands. And whatever it be, may we never neglect an opportunity when they stretch their hand out for ours. I don't know of a better way to spend our pennies.

Resetting Our Default

I knew the question was coming. As soon as I began publishing our pursuit of a more intentional, less screen-saturated life, I knew that readers would ask, "Just how much screen time do you allow?" It's a fair question. We all want to know: How much is too much?

As Gary Chapman points out in *Growing Up Social*, "In terms of how much screen time you allow your child, only you can decide how much is too much."[4] Screen time is a personal choice for every family, and it is not something to be decided or judged by the next family over. It is not our place to judge another parent for their own screen-time limits, or lack thereof. It is our place to set up appropriate boundaries to protect and preserve our own family values.

In a society where one-third of children have a television in their rooms by the time they turn three years old, I knew that any effort I could put into this battle would offer my children a huge advantage. We simply decided to do things differently. We would have one television, and it would be in a central location where we could enjoy a movie together on occasion. Instead of the average forty-two hours a week that a child spends in front of a screen, we would focus on one hour during the week, and maybe a couple of hours on the weekend. That decision alone, although difficult during the first few weeks, would redeem thirty-seven hours a week for our children to spend on more meaningful activities. It would afford us an extra thirty-seven hours every single week to impact our children as we interact with them face-to-face. It's an invaluable gift that we can give our children, by turning off the screens and redeeming back those hours, days, weeks, and a huge bulk of their childhood. It all begins with small choices that hold the power to shift their entire life toward more intentional territory.

To stick to our limits, we made things simple. We would not introduce video games into our home. Our kids would not have free access to our phones or laptops. We would hold off as long as possible on them learning how to operate the remote control—and when they do finally figure it out, they'll understand that it is not at their disposal. Your boundaries will most likely look different; there is no one-size-fits-all model for how screen time should run in a family. Forward progress is what matters as we replace old habits with new activities that nurture a more fulfilling life.

> It's an invaluable gift that we can give our children, by turning off the screens.

Life ebbs and flows with various seasons and an array of needs during those specific times. When a new baby is on the way or has just been welcomed home, when moving into a new home, when a parent is sick, or when Mom just needs an hour to regroup and get dinner on the table—there are places where I believe that a little bit of time in front of the TV is not such a bad thing. In fact, if you knock on our door come Saturday morning, you might just find the kids enjoying some cartoons as my husband and I take our time waking up over hot cups of coffee.

The problem comes when we allow time in front of the screen to become the default. I find that when this becomes the reality in our home, my sons offer me subtle cues as if to tell me through their actions and behaviors that something is off-balance. I see it when they wake in the morning, immediately asking to watch a show. Or when their little hearts are on edge, ready to throw a tantrum or have an emotional meltdown over the tiniest of inconveniences. I can trace back their uncharacteristic behavior to an increase of time in front of a screen. I believe it is a matter of offset. It is not only the actual glow of the screen or entrancement of their attention—it is what that time is stealing away from them. *From us.* As they sit fully engulfed in a device, they are not spending time in my lap, in a book, on the floor, or creating or exploring outside. We lose a lot to these screens. And I believe that it is time we start taking that time back.

Statistics and studies paint a grim picture of children's use of digital devices, but I keep coming around to this conclusion: the last thing parents need is guilt. Taking inventory of how we had spent the past week, I could see that my oldest had been spending an increasing amount of time on the couch in front of our TV. It had become a default reaction to my busyness. He would ask, and I would let out a sigh and reach for the remote control. I was feeling desperate to break the habit we were forming; I knew we needed a creative solution for replacing that screen time with something that would redeem those hours and use them for good.

I had recently purchased a book full of screen-free activities for kids, and decided to give a few of those projects a try. I wrote out a simple list of supplies and headed to the store. That week, I spent time side-by-side with my boys, constructing living-room-sized cities with masking-tape roads for their cars and trucks, complete with bridges and buildings made from recycled boxes. We excavated tiny trucks from blocks of ice using spray bottles, salt, and other various tools. We dyed dry rice and beans with vibrant colors and poured them into a large bin for their trucks to create construction sites out of. As we spent our afternoons on these activities, I would post photos online of our fun together. Yet a part of me was afraid that I would cause that all-too-familiar feeling within other moms that perhaps they were not doing enough. I had felt it myself before, the dangerous act of comparison. As parents, we so easily can have a negative view of our parenthood and believe that we are not doing enough. Not creating enough. Not playing enough. The last thing I wanted to do was heap another ounce of guilt onto another mom.

These activities that my boys and I were doing had two prerequisites. First, they could not require a lot of money. Second, they could not require a lot of prep time. It was not that I was slaving away creating these perfectly planned out crafts and projects. I wanted something that would be quick, simple, and cheap, and focused on imagination. The other piece of honesty that I hoped to convey was that I wasn't creating these activities because I was the best mom on the block, always providing my kids with endless creative ventures. No, the reason I was dying rice and making cities from masking tape was because I was trying to fix something. My boys had been watching too much TV, and this was a simple solution to something I had let get out of hand.

What I discovered through these activities was little less than extraordinary. I saw it as I sat back on the couch, watching our middle son race his off-road truck from our parking lot made of a cereal box toward the bridge made from a plastic-wrap box. When the week before I would have clicked on their latest favorite TV show, today I spent five minutes on my knees running tape from one side of the room to the other. And that simple decision, along with a tiny investment of money and time, gifted them with hours of imaginative play instead of time in front of the TV. Before I knew it, within just a couple of weeks, the boys had stopped asking to watch TV and were coming up with their own games and activities on their own initiation. It was a lot easier than I anticipated, and wildly rewarding.

It brought me back to that same conclusion—the last thing parents need is guilt. Really, all we need is a little bit of inspiration and some creative ideas. What if all we needed to reclaim the weeks of our children's lives was a small shift in our parenting approach, and just a bit of intentionality? I was surprised by how little was required in redirecting my children's days and making the most of our days at home together. My eyes were opened to the truth that what we parents need is not another book telling us that we are doing things wrong and that our children will suffer for it. No, what we need is a solution and a bit of hope. What would happen if we all caught a glimpse of how different our and our children's lives could be if we began reclaiming that time one hour of play at a time? Perhaps it is one of the richest gifts we could ever give our children.

I have found that when it comes to setting up screen-time boundaries, it helps to focus on what we are gaining rather than what we are losing. When I began limiting my boys' screen time, a part of me mourned losing that dependable source of entertainment for them, and a break for me. But that mourning lasted only a short time as I began to catch a glimpse of all that we were gaining through this decision, and that it was well worth the sacrifice. I gained more significant one-on-one time with them. They gained more time playing outside and creating things with their hands. We all gained greater clarity in our minds and hearts of what truly matters in life, and how our hearts long to spend the time we have been given.

Every time I choose to sit down and read books with my children, my heart feels fuller and my relationship grows stronger with them. Every time I choose to spend ten minutes pushing them on the tire swing or playing kickball in the backyard, those end up being the most memorable pieces of our day. And every single time we make one of those intentional choices, they become more and more a part of our families and the culture of our homes.

When we say *no* to screens ruling our children's lives, we say *yes* to so much more. We say *yes* to opportunities for them to practice affection, appreciation, apology, and attention[5]—virtues that the screen does not afford them, but that they will need more and more as they grow.

We say *yes* to training them how to be successful adults who value relationships. We say *yes* to laughter, eye contact, and teamwork. Yes to creativity, ingenuity, and problem solving. *Yes* to boredom, which opens up to them worlds of opportunity. We say *yes* to giving them a life made up of things that truly matter.

Questions to Reflect On

- What specific questions can you ask yourself to stay in check with your technology use? Make a list and revisit it often. Perhaps post it above your work desk or as a background image on your laptop.

- Watch your children this week and keep a simple list of what their hands are occupied with. What are your own hands busy with, and what is this communicating to your child?

- What small decisions could you make in order to offer your child a less screen-saturated childhood? Wherever you are coming from, give yourself grace. Write down one next step or goal and make it happen this week.

-ten-
Timeless

"Be Brave, Little One"

I was ten years old when I got caught up in the clouds. I spent many evenings of my childhood riding in our car during thunderstorms. It was my father's idea. Whenever lightning was on the horizon, he would call us into the front screen porch to watch it drift in, warning of power and danger. Then he would often load our family into the car to chase the storm, reliving his storm-chasing days in college. My siblings would tease me not to touch the metal clasps of my seatbelt, in case the car was struck by lightning and I would be electrocuted. I pulled my little hands quickly into my lap.

I never told my dad I was terrified of the storms, that every time the thunder rolled I would whisper a prayer that our home would not be taken up in a tornado. Despite my fear, intrigue began to take over and I developed an intense interest in weather. I assembled my own weather-watching kit, and every afternoon I would sit on our front porch and document the temperatures and the types of clouds floating adrift in the sky. It was that year that my dad took me to a storm-spotters class. I sat for a whole morning surrounded by adults, learning how to identify weather patterns and potential threats of danger. By the end of the day, at age ten, I was a trained storm spotter.

A year later, at age eleven, my hands held firmly to the black plastic of a camera—steady, strong, aim, focus. The wings of the butterfly fluttered nervously as I neared. All around me adults wandered through the grassy yard in search of interesting subjects to bring into focus. I didn't notice them; I was alone with the butterfly, ready for the capture—not a literal capture, but an image capture. I was in practice. In twenty minutes we would all retreat inside to enjoy lunch together. My father had packed me my own sandwich—Swiss cheese and pepperoni on white bread.

That morning we had driven six hours, beginning before the sun came up, and our first stop had been at a little cafe in a tourist town. I had eaten there half a dozen times in my short lifetime, all while on vacation to this dream place of my childhood. We came every year, sometimes twice, to the wooded retreat of Door County, Wisconsin.

Every time before, we had come as a family and stayed for at least a week. Today, however, it was my father and me, and only for a day. We would drive back home that evening, but the day was about us—he was pouring into me. He had always had an interest in photography, and I had caught that interest. As I began to pick up cameras, he didn't tell me to carefully set them back down. Instead, he let me ponder them, click buttons, practice. And now today we had ventured out to a photography class. I was the only child in a classroom of adults learning to capture moments. This day would become a moment captured in my own soul, one of my father and me, and his investment in my interests.

I was twelve years old when my parents, picking up on my interest in becoming a veterinarian when I grew up, encouraged me to ask the local vet clinic if I could come in to volunteer in any way. The clinic offered to have me come in once a week to shadow one of the veterinarians. Every week all summer long I woke early, slipped on medical scrubs decorated with rainbow-colored cats that my mother had bought for me, and spent my morning petting distraught dogs and watching cats get declawed. It didn't take too many observations of cats going under the knife and being spayed for me to realize that I was not, after all, cut out to be an animal doctor—or any kind of doctor for that matter. My parents hadn't just said, "Oh, that's nice, honey," when I mentioned the idea of being a veterinarian. They went a step further and directed me in how I might pursue my interests—and that left a lasting mark on me, one that would influence my own parenting years down the road.

I was thirteen when my dad set me up on a stool in the musty work room he had created in our basement. We opened the package of the model Grand Prix car, unadorned and full of potential. I had my doubts—we had begun this process late. The race was approaching, and here my car sat unassembled as a block of wood. As he always did, my father began to divulge knowledge before we ever began the process. He explained the techniques that would give my car an advantage in the race. We would raise one wheel slightly to lessen the friction of plastic wheel against wooden race course. We would assemble it as close to the weight limit as we could, giving the car the most momentum possible to carry it speedily down the course. And then, on the day of, at the final weigh-in we would drill additional weights on until it was right on the mark of the weight limit. I imagined the ugly screws sticking out of my car, that would, hopefully by then, look beautiful. I decided to trust him. We won that race.

I was fifteen years old when my mom rented out a table at a local craft fair. I was headed to Thailand that summer on a missions trip, and I had a lot of money to raise. My mom and I spent hours side by side working on crafts and preparing for the sale. When fair day came, we sold very little, not even enough to pay for the table space we rented, and yet I remember that time fondly because my mom believed in me and invested her time and money into my ideas and passions.

My parents were "yes" parents. This did not mean that they said *yes* to our every request or catered to everything we wanted to do. Rather, it meant that they had attuned their hearts to picking up on our interests and took the time to pay attention to our ideas. Not only did they say *yes* when we wanted to pursue an interest, they also identified those interests within us and drew them out, encouraging and equipping us to gain knowledge and pursue those passions. Although I still enjoy capturing moments through photography today, I no longer chase storms or build winning Grand Prix cars (although I'm sure that is in my future, as a mom of boys).

Something powerful happens when we recognize a child's interest and take the time to invest in it. When we encourage them in their pursuits, they gain confidence. They become brave. Whether or not they stick with those interests into adulthood, that bravery will stick with them. The confidence we give them right now will flourish and thrive as they make big choices as an adult. When our child comes to us with their latest idea, and we take the time to stop, give credit to their creativity, and equip them with what they need to chase that idea, we are in essence telling them, *Be brave, little one.*

This can be very difficult to do, I understand, if you yourself did not grow up in a home where your interests and ideas were listened to and respected.

How can you offer your child confidence when you yourself are held back by insecurities? We have to view it like this: When we gift our children with our attention and we give merit to their ideas and interests, we ourselves are growing as an individual and as a parent. We need to be willing to step out and do something unfamiliar. It might begin by sitting down and listening to his plan for that latest treehouse construction, or purchasing some supplies for the crafts she wants sell at the upcoming craft fair.

> Something powerful happens when we recognize a child's interest and take the time to invest in it.

By investing ourselves in our child's interests, we infuse their growing spirit with the confidence to chase after that which might be a little bit scary and a lot unknown. And just imagine what they'll make of their lives when we gift them with that kind of bravery.

Those jars with their 936 pennies hold so much potential for the time we have with our children. Yet they hold endless potential for the time after, when our children are grown and chasing after their own dreams. With these 936 weeks, we can set them up to live lives packed full of meaningful pursuits, equipped with the confidence we spoke into them as children. Some of the greatest gifts we can offer our children during our 936 weeks are those gifts that will continue giving long after those pennies are spent.

Supermoons and Small Love

We were driving higher into the mountains. With each bend of the road we raced the setting of the sun and the moon's ascent. It was to be a supermoon, unrivaled in size or brightness for the past sixty-nine years. For the past 25,130 days, the moon had climbed the horizon and hung in the sky, but never with this much awe and majesty.

As soon as my husband had returned home from work, we piled the boys into the car and set out to find the perfect spot to watch the scene unfold. My husband pulled off into a small gravel parking lot, backing us into a spot next to a handful of other cars holding an eager audience. Memories flooded back to me of my own childhood and the late night excursions my dad had taken us on to go watch the northern lights or catch a meteor shower. They were unforgettable memories for me, fibers woven into the woman I am today. And here we were about to create those very same kind of memories with our own children.

We opened the back hatch of our SUV and sat the boys down to wait and watch. Only, sitting and waiting is hardly what they did. We could see the faint glow, a reflection off the clouds as the moon slowly made its way up from behind the foothill in front of us. The glow grew brighter and brighter, and so did the boys' rowdiness. The couple leaning against the car next to ours smiled at the boys, then turned their attention back to the moon. I was thankful to have the dark of the night to hide the flush of embarrassment on my face as our boy jumped about. "Zeke, quiet down. Sit down. Watch. You won't see the moon again like this until you're big like Daddy." He glanced at the massive orange orb for a moment, then turned back to his antics. My anger rose right along with the moon.

Sometimes we want things to be just right, so much so that a bit of inconvenience can threaten to spoil the entirety of a memory. Have you ever become so preoccupied with a preconceived notion of what a memory should be made of that you throw the entire experience out at the slightest hurdle? That is how I felt on this evening, hushing my boys and trying to enjoy this rare experience with them. But then something struck me as I stared at that breathtaking moon casting its brilliant glow against the night sky. The foothills were painted as a silhouette in the glow, and a dozen planes blinked against the darkness of the night as they drifted into the airport down in the city. The sight was stunning. But when I gazed upon the scene with all of its brilliance, I had this thought: The One who created such magnificence and called it good called us, His children, *very good.* He created us with more mastery and creativity and beauty than even this moon in all of its splendor.

> Have you ever become so preoccupied with a preconceived notion of what a memory should be made of that you throw the entire experience out at the slightest hurdle?

This slightly cranky, misbehaved, impatient, and messy scene of a family in our SUV held more magnificence than the peaceful, tranquil, mesmerizing scene before me. God called the moon good. He calls my family *very* good. And He does the same for yours.

When we are at our ugliest—when tempers flare and expectations are not met—God calls us beautiful, the favorite of all of His creation. All of the brilliance of creation doesn't hold a candle to the wonder He breathes into His children. Suddenly I saw my boys and their imperfections—along with my own—in a very different light, one that beamed brighter than any supermoon ever would.

That evening, after we returned home, our two younger boys went to bed early. Our oldest, upon finishing his dinner, climbed up into my lap on the couch. The day had been long and he had thoroughly tested my patience. I told him it was bedtime; he cuddled closer. "I just want you for a little bit longer," he said, his voice muffled as his face pressed into my side. I wrapped my arms around him, and there we sat for a good long while. As he lay there on top of me, I was taken aback by how he hardly fit into my embrace anymore; his body sprawled across me. His breathing grew longer and more calm as the whole of him relaxed into me. When was the last time I studied his eyelashes, the ones that captivated me when he was a nursing newborn? His face was sun-kissed from hours out in the yard, and I noticed the small scar on his right cheek from when he fell out of a tree earlier in the summer. He looked up at me and smiled, completely content in my gaze. He fingered the necklace hanging on my neck. "What do all of these letters say, Mom?" I'm not much of a jewelry wearer, but I had fallen in love with the necklace at an auction for a dear friend raising money to bring her adopted son home from Africa. Rather, I fell in love with the words encapsulated within it. *Refuse Small Love*, it reads. I ran my fingers through his hair. "It means that I need to love you well, with all my heart."

That evening we could have stayed home. The day had been trying, and I was exhausted. When my husband came home, I was donning dirty sweatpants and an old T-shirt, my hair tossed up in the same frazzled ponytail that I had rolled out of bed with that morning. "I think I went to the store like this," I'd admitted to him. The idea of chasing the moon sounded altogether romantic, but it was a toss-up with the day we'd had. We could have stayed home. But we chose to go and offer our children an experience they won't have a chance at again until all of those pennies in our jars are spent. We chose a bigger kind of love that stands unmoved in the face of inconvenience. Small love asks, "Why bother?" Or, in the face of inconvenience and plans gone awry, it says, "That was a waste." Refusing small love, and embracing big love, looks like overlooking offense, shrugging off inconvenience, and offering our loved ones the gift of our presence.

That is what these penny jars are all about—choosing big love over small love. Big love requires our full presence, our undivided attention, our dedicated resolve, and our full surrender. After all, we can offer none of these things unless our hearts are surrendered to God's bigger plans and purposes for our families.

Investing these pennies is about trusting in those bigger plans and being faithful to show up ready for the journey. I am sure, looking back years from now when our pennies are spent, that my boy will remember not the glow of the supermoon that night, but the linger of my embrace as we laid together on the couch—an act of refusing small love. And one more penny invested in a brighter future for him.

The Full Jar

After I first wrote of our little penny jar, I received many responses from parents whose jars were already empty—all spent up. It got me thinking about my own jar, those 936 pennies spent on me by my own parents, and how I do not see that jar empty at all. Rather, I see it full.

When I was nine, my mom offered me a few small words during our homeschool studies that ended up being anything but small. The assignment was to write a short story. I wrote of a man. He stood in the cabin of a ship, beside a small bed with an end table sitting next to it. Atop the end table was a photo that the man stared at. It was a photo of himself and his family. The photo was hugged by a wooden frame; not the cheap kind of wooden frame you buy from the Dollar Store, but real wood, with grain that the man could feel under his fingertips when he picked up the photo to admire it more closely.

It began in the cabin of that ship, with the man smoothing his fingers along the grain of the wooden frame, gazing at his family. It began when I was a child, my stocking feet planted firmly on the wood flooring we had installed as a family the week we bought our home. My mom sat quietly at the table as she read my story. She complimented me on my writing style. And I don't know if she remembers that day, or my story, or knows that I was a little bit nervous as I stood there watching her read my work. I don't remember her exact words, but whatever they were, they shaped me. They set me on a road that would eventually lead me to one of the things I am most passionate about, the thing God uses in my life daily to show me myself and himself: sharing God's grace and my story through words. My mother's words on that ordinary day, whatever they were, they told me to keep going. And so I did. Her words that day were a penny well spent. They were a choice she made on one ordinary day to set me up to see my life years later—*to really see it*, take it in, understand it, enjoy it, and share it.

My jar of pennies is full of these kinds of memories, of choices and adventures and values that my parents chose to gift me with. They spoke into my siblings and me words of confidence, and they loved us with deep, unconditional love that served as a firm foundation for our childhood and adulthood.

As a mother myself now, I am sure that my parents look back on those weeks of raising my sister, my brother, and me, and I'm certain they have their own questions about how that time was spent. They have their own doubts and regrets. And yet, as their grown child, what I see looking back is all the time that they invested in us. This helps me to see my own parenthood in a more gracious light, knowing that despite my failures and regrets, whatever I pour into making memories, slowing time, and preserving our moments to hand off as a legacy—that is what my children will remember and be thankful for.

When the pennies of my childhood were all spent and I packed up my Jeep with photos, empty notebooks, bedding, and a few dollars and set off down the highway toward college and my adult life, my parents understood that although the jar was empty, there was another jar now full—invested with the weeks that they had poured into me since my birth. And those pennies would serve as a firm foundation and navigational beacon for me now as I managed my adult life. How my parents chose to invest the pennies of my childhood gives me great hope, confidence, and wisdom for how to invest the pennies in my own children's jars. And I pray that my husband and I will hand off the same kind of jar of pennies to our boys after our 936 weeks are invested.

I understand that many of you reading these words are in a very different place. Maybe, like many stories I read after I published the 936 Pennies blog post, your pennies are all spent and your heart aches with regret of opportunities lost, a child gone astray, or time you can never get back. Maybe you are like the mother I spoke with whose daughter, despite their greatest efforts, chose a way they would have never hoped for her. After years of no communication, this mother wrote her daughter a letter. She never knew whether her daughter read it, but regardless, the letter provided deep healing for this mother. It released her from those questions that haunted her about her penny-spending, time-investing efforts. With the sending of that letter, she found room to breathe and move on.

Wherever you are in your penny-spending journey, hope is not lost. If your jar stands on that shelf full of copper coins and po-tential, your baby swaddled in her bassinet, then know that those pennies beg to be well spent. And also know that we are never guaranteed the whole of them, so we must invest each one with our full presence and big love.

If you're like me and you're staring at those penny jars partly spent, begging them to *please just slow down*, take a moment to picture that second jar. Remember that when our 936 pennies are all spent, there will be another jar now full, packed with memories and legacy to carry our children through adulthood.

If your jars are half spent, or even empty, and you're lament-ing the opportunities you never took, the pennies lost among the couch cushions, or the hurt that has left tarnish on those coins, there is hope. Maybe it's time to take a good look at your family's lifestyle, determine what your family values are, and begin shifting your penny-spending toward more intentional territory. It might be time to write a letter of apology. It might be time to call a family meeting and hold a difficult conversation, one that holds the power to redirect the course of your family's legacy. Maybe it's time to make a hard phone call and speak some hope into those pennies already spent, redeeming them with healing words of apology.

And if you never had the chance to spend your pennies, if they were taken from you long before you ever anticipated, and your jar and heart lay empty and aching, know that your child's story matters. Those pennies, whether you got to spend two hundred of them, twenty, or none, they mattered. A penny jar never, ever goes to waste, because every single life matters.

No matter how the 936 pennies of your own childhood were spent, you have the choice and power to spend your child's pennies well. You have the opportunity to shift a legacy and change a family history.

So, dear friend, on your time-investing journey, let us all be wise in our penny spending, because the days are short. Time is fleeting. Tomorrow is never promised. Legacies are made today. And that is exactly what we do have: today. These jars are never meant to evoke guilt. They are meant to speak hope into the deepest parts of us. They are meant to constantly remind us that *today matters*. Yesterday is done, tomorrow is a new opportunity. Today is what we have right now, so let's invest it well. Today we can choose to sink our feet deep into the moments, offering them our full attention and presence. Today we have the opportunity to speak truth, gift confidence, hug long, laugh loud, and love big. And that right there is a penny well spent.

And so, dear friend, here is to counting time, and making time count.

Acknowledgments

There are so many whom God used in beautiful ways to bring the message of *936 Pennies* to the bookshelves. I am indebted to so many for their unceasing encouragement, assistance, and prayers.

Thank you first and foremost to our Father God, who's hand was at work in the details from the very beginning. This project and message was first and always His.

Thank you to my husband, Grayson, who told me I could do this, and never let me forget or doubt that. I would rather no one else by my side to spend these pennies with.

Thank you to my peer review team: each of you eagerly embraced this message from the beginning, and have offered your invaluable insights and prayers. Your prayers carried this project through.

Thank you to Fellowship of Grace and Pastor Michael for our very first jar of 936 pennies. Your ministry to parents and families is a beautiful testimony to God's grace and plan.

Thank you to HACWN, my first community of writers. Thank you to Les for being used by God to spread His messages, including this one, and for your willingness to work with first-time authors. Thank you to Bethany House for being used by God to make this happen.

Thank you to Abbigail for your gracious editing all the way through. Thank you to Dawn for believing in me, cheering me on, and praying for me over cups of coffee. Thank you to Hannah, Biz, Chris, Arlene, and Dawn for your insights and additions. Your feedback shaped this book.

Thank you to my dad, Alan, and my mom, Arlene, for modeling to me through the 936 weeks of my own childhood what wise spending looks like. You taught me the richest ways to invest time. I am forever grateful.

Notes

Chapter 3: Slowing Time

1. Serena B. Miller, *More Than Happy* (New York: Howard Books, 2015), 283.
2. Rachel Macy Stafford, *Hands Free Life* (Grand Rapids, MI: Zondervan, 2015), 12–13.
3. Watchman Nee, *Sit, Walk, Stand* (Fort Washington, PA: CLC Publications, 2009 edition), 16.
4. Ann Kroeker and Charity Singleton Craig, *On Being a Writer* (New York: T. S. Poetry Press, 2014), 49.

Chapter 4: Speaking of Time

1. Brené Brown, *Daring Greatly* (New York: Penguin, 2012), 72.

Chapter 6: A Perspective on Time

1. Lisa-Jo Baker, *Surprised by Motherhood* (Carol Stream, IL: Tyndale, 2014), 93.
2. Kayla Aimee, *Anchored* (Nashville: B&H Publishing, 2015), 118.

Chapter 7: Navigating Time

1. Tedd Tripp, *Shepherding a Child's Heart* (Wapwallopen, PA: Shepherd Press, 1995), 41.

Chapter 8: Preserving Time

1. Kroeker and Craig, *On Being a Writer*, 48.
2. Baker, *Surprised by Motherhood*, 116–117.

Chapter 9: Buying Back Time

1. Statistic derived from https://www.commonsensemedia.org/the-common-sense-census-media-use-by-tweens-and-teens-infographic# and Padma Ravichandran, "Young Children and Screen Time," National Center for Health Research, https://www.center4research.org/young-children-screen-time-tv-computers-etc/.

2. Gary Chapman and Arlene Pellicane, *Growing Up Social* (Chicago: Northfield Publishing, 2014), 16.

3. Stafford, *Hands Free Life*, 157.

4. Chapman and Pellicane, *Growing Up Social*, 19.

5. These four A's come from Chapman and Pellicane, *Growing Up Social*.

Eryn Lynum lives in northern Colorado with her husband and three boys, where they spend their time hiking, camping, and exploring the Rocky Mountains. Her work and passion is to come alongside of authors and help them market the message God has laid on their hearts. She loves to travel and share at conferences, churches, and writers' groups. But every opportunity she gets, she is out exploring God's creation with her family.